GETTING STARTED WITH ANCIENT GREEK

Beginning Classical/New Testament Greek
for Homeschoolers and Self-Taught
Students of Any Age

WILLIAM E. LINNEY

ARMFIELD ACADEMIC PRESS

Published by Armfield Academic Press

Editorial consultants: Jenni Glaser, Michael D. Sweet, Katherine L. Bradshaw, Michelle Yancich, Andrew Morehouse

Editorial assistant: Ben Turnbull

ISBN: 978-1-62611-017-5

CONTENTS

PREFACE...iv

HOW TO USE THIS BOOK...vi

LESSONS 1–158...1

ANSWER KEY...232

THE GREEK ALPHABET GUIDE......................................249

GREEK DIPHTHONGS...250

GLOSSARY..251

PREFACE

My first book, *Getting Started with Latin,* was a labor of love. I wrote it to help homeschooled and self-taught students learn beginning Latin at home, without a teacher. Since the publication of *Getting Started with Latin,* the response has been positive (except for that one nasty email I got a few years back). People seem to like the one-thing-at-a-time format of the book, which never leaves them lost and wondering what just happened like other books do. This is significant because homeschooled and self-taught students are a special group of people who need specialized materials—products that allow them to learn at home without access to a teacher who specializes in that particular subject.

Since writing *Getting Started with Latin,* I have written books about Spanish, French, and German. But I have always wanted to write a beginning ancient Greek book that follows the same method as *Getting Started with Latin.* And now, after a few years of slow development, it's finally finished.

Getting Started with Ancient Greek is designed to accomplish several educational goals. I have designed this book to...

- Be self-explanatory, self-paced, self-contained, and inexpensive
- Allow the student to make progress with or without a teacher
- Provide plenty of practice exercises after each new concept so that the student can master each idea before moving on to the next one
- Provide audio recordings for aural practice and supplementary instruction
- Avoid making ancient Greek any more difficult than it actually is

Getting Started with Ancient Greek was created to meet the unique needs of homeschooled and self-taught students. It is self-contained, with no extra materials to purchase (such as pronunciation recordings, answer keys, or teachers' editions). It's also in a large format to make it easier to use, and non-consumable (that is, you don't write in it) so it can be used with multiple children. The answer key is in the back of the book, and there are free pronunciation recordings and author's commentary recordings available at the following website:

www.GettingStartedWithAncientGreek.com

In this book, new words and concepts are introduced in a gradual yet systematic fashion. Each lesson provides many exercises for practicing the new material while reviewing material from previous lessons.

Getting Started with Ancient Greek makes ancient Greek accessible to students of any age or educational background. Because this book moves so gradually, you probably will not say *This is too hard for me. I quit!* Instead, these bite-size lessons leave you encouraged and ready to continue. But when you do finish this book, don't let your Greek studies end there. Learning and using a foreign language is quite a thrill—so keep going, and above all, have fun with it!

William E. Linney

HOW TO USE THIS BOOK

This book is structured around one main teaching method: Teach one concept at a time and let the student master that concept before introducing the next one. With that in mind, read the tips listed below to help you use this book to the greatest advantage.

WHAT KIND OF GREEK IS THIS?

People who study ancient Greek generally fall into two broad categories: 1) those who want to study the Greek New Testament and 2) those who want to study classical Greek writers such as Plato, Aristotle, and Herodotus—or perhaps the epic poems of Homer. Therefore, depending on what kind of Greek you want to learn, you may be wondering whether or not this is the right book for you. Here's the answer: the ancient Greek presented in this book is so basic that this book can be used as an introduction to whatever flavor of ancient Greek you would like to study. In this book we will focus on the absolute basics of the language, building a foundation for any future ancient Greek studies.

THE NEW WORD

Start each lesson by observing the new word for that particular lesson. All Greek words in this book are, of course, in the Greek alphabet. The meaning of the new word is in *italics*. In some lessons you will learn a new concept along with the new word, while in others you will simply review material from previous lessons.

A NOTE ON TYPOGRAPHY

I have taken great care to make the Greek words in this book as legible as possible (unlike some other Greek textbooks) by using a large font size and by increasing the boldness of the font slightly. Also, I have made sure that there is plenty of space between lines of Greek text, between Greek letters, and between Greek words. My philosophy is simple: the more legible the Greek text is, the easier it will be for you to learn.

PRONUNCIATION

The best way to learn ancient Greek pronunciation is by listening to it and copying what you hear. Be sure to visit

www.GettingStartedWithAncientGreek.com

to access the free pronunciation recordings that accompany this book. You may listen to these audio recordings on YouTube or you may download the recordings directly onto your device in MP3 format. In these free recordings, each word and exercise is read aloud so you can learn how everything sounds and practice your Greek listening skills, too. You may play these recordings on any device you wish, including a computer, smart phone, or tablet.

If the new word for a certain lesson is difficult to pronounce, that lesson will have a written description of how to pronounce the new word (that's the part of the lesson called "Pronunciation Tip"). The purpose of these tips is not to tell you exactly how that word sounds—instead, it's to give you a general idea of how the word sounds and to help you avoid common pronunciation errors. Also, there is a pronunciation chart at the end of the book for reference.

SPEAK THE LANGUAGE

If I could recommend any one particular thing that could help you learn ancient Greek faster and more easily, it would be to speak the language every day. Yes, you read that correctly—I said to speak ancient Greek. The Greek language has been continuously spoken for thousands of years, so don't be afraid to open your mouth and speak some Greek!

If you only read Greek and translate it into English, your experience with Greek will be limited. When you translate Greek, here is the sequence of events: 1) You see a Greek word. 2) You try to think of the English equivalent of that word. 3) When the English equivalent pops into your head, it brings with it the meanings, thoughts, and feelings associated with it. This kind of exercise really is focused on English, not Greek, because the goal becomes to get the English words right. Sure, you start out with Greek, but everything ends up as English.

But when you speak Greek, your mind remains focused on Greek. Since you can't depend on English to express yourself verbally, you must keep the Greek words you know in the forefront of your mind, using them to formulate thoughts and to create meaningful sentences. And as you speak Greek more and more, you will begin to associate images, thoughts, and feelings with the Greek words themselves, not just with their English equivalents. This will help you to form a more direct, intimate connection with the Greek language.

So as you go through this book, don't just read and translate the exercises—also incorporate speaking and listening into your daily study habits. There are several ways to do this. One way is to have conversations in Greek with another person such as a teacher, parent, family member, or fellow student. You can talk about the things that happen in the exercises in the book, or you can do role-playing exercises in which you pretend to be one of the people in the exercises. If you have no one to talk to, don't worry—you can still do something called *narration*. Narration is, more or less, talking to yourself. You can read some exercises in Greek and then begin to talk about them out loud in Greek, retelling or restating what happened. You can pretend to be one of the characters in the exercises and speak in the first person. Pretend that you are speaking to someone else in the second person, or talking about someone else in the third person. Another useful technique is to close your eyes and see the story in your mind's eye while you narrate what is happening in Greek. Some language learners practice by speaking to their pets—the family cat won't mind listening to you for a few minutes between naps. At a bare minimum, you can repeat the exercises out loud or even try to recite them from memory. The idea here is to somehow get you saying something in ancient Greek every day.

Above all, don't think of ancient Greek as a museum exhibit that sits inside a glass display case—something that can only be looked at but never touched or handled. Instead, try to view it as something that you can pick up, touch, examine—even play with. Don't be afraid to make mistakes! Mistakes are an important part of the learning process. Roll up your sleeves and jump fully into the ancient Greek language, and you will experience the language in a more fulfilling and satisfying way.

GRAMMATICAL INFORMATION

If needed, a lesson may contain an explanation of how to use the new word introduced in that lesson. Charts and examples are used to give the reader a clear presentation of the grammatical knowledge needed for that particular lesson.

The book's website has special audio commentary recordings which have been prepared by the author. These recordings discuss each lesson, so if you have any trouble understanding the material presented in a lesson, you will have plenty of help on hand.

THE EXERCISES

Armed with knowledge of the new word and how to use it, begin to translate the exercises. In a homeschool environment, it is probably best to have students write their answers in a notebook. Older students and adults may prefer to do the exercises mentally. Next, turn to the answer key to see if your translations are correct. In the paperback version of the book, the answer key is in the back. In the Kindle version, the answers are immediately after the lesson, on the next page. By comparing the exercises and the answers, you will learn from your mistakes. Translating the exercises over and over (even memorizing them) will enhance learning and speed your progress. After you have translated the exercises and you know what they mean, listen to the audio recordings over and over for practice. The more you listen, the faster your progress will be.

REPEATED LISTENING

After you have studied the exercises and you know what they mean, you are in a position to use an extremely effective language learning technique. This technique involves reading or hearing understandable material in the foreign language that you are studying. If you are studying a foreign language, and you hear or read lots of material that you can't understand, it doesn't really do you any good. But if you hear or read something that is at your current level of learning, you are getting some good practice interpreting that language because the material is understandable.

Here's how this applies to you: once you have studied the exercises for a certain lesson, and you know what the exercises mean, you should listen to the audio recordings for that lesson over and over. Don't just listen once or twice—listen to them a hundred times, until everything you hear sounds natural to you. Listen in the car, while cleaning up, etc. This study method will help your brain to process, absorb, and get used to the language.

GREEK COMPOSITION

For an additional challenge, you can try to translate the answers in the answer key back into Greek using the knowledge you have gained from that lesson. This is a great learning tool because it requires you to approach the material from a completely different direction. Try it and see! Again, it is probably best to write these exercises in a notebook.

DON'T PUT THE CART BEFORE THE HORSE

Do not skip ahead to a future lesson. Because each lesson builds directly on the preceding lessons, do the lessons in the order given. If you start to feel lost or confused, back up a few lessons and review. Or, take a break and come back to the material at a later time. Remember that review and repetition are essential when learning any language. One of the best things you can do to improve your understanding of this language is to review the lessons repeatedly.

STAY FLEXIBLE

Everyone has a different learning style, so use this book in ways that fit your needs or the needs of your students. You can learn as a family, on your own, or in a homeschool environment. Be creative! You could even have one night of the week when the entire family is forbidden to speak English! Who knows? You may think of a way to use this book that no one else has thought of (putting it under the short leg of the kitchen table does not count).

TESTS AND QUIZZES

To give a student a test or quiz, simply back up to a previous lesson and have the student translate those exercises without looking at the answers. Then, the teacher or parent can grade the exercises using the answers in the back of the book. Another possibility would be to test the student's listening skills by having the student translate the exercises directly from the audio recording for that lesson.

SCHEDULING

Some homeschool parents like a lot of structure in their teaching schedules, while others prefer a less structured learning environment. Depending on your personal preferences, you may either plan to cover a certain number of lessons in a certain period of time, or allow your students to determine their own pace. It's up to you.

HOW MUCH TIME PER DAY?

A few minutes a day with this book is better than longer, less frequent sessions. Thirty minutes a day is ideal for language study. Of course, this may vary with each student's age, ability, and interest level.

SELF-TAUGHT ADULTS

Adults who use this book will enjoy the freedom of learning whenever and wherever they please. High school and college students may use it to get a head start before taking a traditional class at their school, to satisfy curiosity, or to try something new. Busy adults may use it to study at lunchtime, break time, or while commuting to work (as long as someone else is driving the vehicle). The short lessons in this book will fit any schedule.

SURF THE INTERWEBS!

Don't forget about the website that accompanies this book. Here's that web address again, in case you missed it:

www.GettingStartedWithAncientGreek.com

It has free resources to aid you in your studies. Be sure to check it out!

LESSON ONE

THE GREEK ALPHABET AND YOU

Languages start out as spoken words, not as written texts. If you want to write down a language, you'll need some kind of writing system. As English speakers, we write down our language with an alphabet. Each letter makes a different sound, and we can use these letters to spell out the words of our language.

Just for fun, here's a quick overview of how our alphabet developed (use the numbers to follow along with the map of the Mediterranean Sea that is provided below). It all started way back in ancient Egypt, the land of the pyramids and the Nile river (1). The Egyptians used special symbols called *hieroglyphs* to write the Egyptian language on statues, monuments, and on the walls of tombs and temples. It's a long story, but some of these Egyptian characters were used to create an early alphabet for languages related to Hebrew. Archaeologists have found inscriptions using this early alphabet in the Sinai Peninsula (2). This early alphabet traveled to Palestine (3) where it was used by various groups of people. The Phoenicians were sea merchants who were based in what today would be Lebanon (4). As they sailed all over the Mediterranean Sea, they took this alphabet with them. The ancient Greeks (5) borrowed this alphabet from the Phoenicians, made a few changes, and used it to write down the ancient Greek language. The Romans (6), with some help from their Etruscan neighbors, adapted the Greek alphabet for

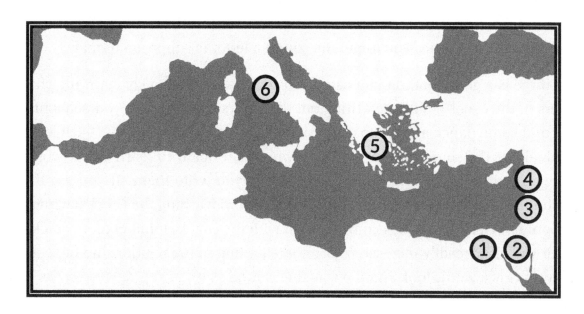

Latin. The Romans then spread the Latin language and their alphabet throughout Europe. As a result, many European languages are written today with the Roman alphabet—languages such as Spanish, French, English, Italian, German, and various Scandinavian languages. Today, we call this alphabet the Latin alphabet, although sometimes you will see it called the Roman alphabet.

Here's what all this means to you as a beginning student of Greek: You need to learn the letters of the Greek alphabet. As an English speaker, you already have a head start because, as I just mentioned, the Greek alphabet is related to the Latin alphabet. For this reason, some of the letters of the Greek alphabet will look familiar to you, but other letters won't. So your first task in learning Greek is to learn the Greek alphabet. And that's the purpose of the first part of this book—to teach you the letters of the Greek alphabet one by one.

LESSON TWO

WRITE THE LETTERS

Learning to read a new alphabet can be quite a challenge—it can feel as if you are a beginning reader, learning to read for the first time. In order to read Greek, your eye must learn to recognize each letter quickly, and you must remember the pronunciation of each letter so you can sound out words. And when you're starting out, sometimes you forget the sound a letter is supposed to make!

But there is a good method you can use to help yourself quickly learn the characters of the Greek alphabet: writing out the letters by hand. Get yourself a nice pen and some paper, and try to copy each letter exactly. As you write each letter, think about the sound it makes. Later, when you begin to learn Greek words, write out entire words and pronounce them as you write them. If you use this method regularly, it will speed your progress toward learning the Greek language. Not only will it help you to become familiar with the Greek alphabet more quickly, but it will also steadily increase your understanding of the relationship between the way Greek words look and the way they sound.

LESSON THREE

As a speaker and reader of the English language, you are accustomed to seeing uppercase and lowercase forms of each letter. Sometimes the uppercase form and lowercase form of a letter look very similar, as seen with the letter *w*.

W w

But with other letters, the uppercase and lowercase forms can look very different, as seen with the letter *g*:

G g

And it's the same way with the Greek alphabet. Each Greek letter has an uppercase and lowercase form. Sometimes the uppercase and lowercase forms will look similar, but other times they won't.

Actually, the ancient Greeks didn't even have uppercase and lowercase letters. The only letters they had were the ones that we would call uppercase—that is, the letters that they borrowed from the Phoenicians. But later, in the Middle Ages, scribes developed lowercase forms of each letter to make it easier for them to copy Greek texts by hand. When the printing press was invented and they began to print Greek texts, they did not revert back to using only uppercase Greek letters. Instead, they made the printed letters look like the lowercase letter style that the scribes had developed. And that's still the way ancient Greek texts are printed today (as you will see in this book). But uppercase Greek letters haven't been abandoned—you will still see capital letters at the beginning of the name of a person or place, the same as you would in English. The first word of a sentence, however, is not usually capitalized in modern editions of Greek texts.

LESSON FOUR

TWO FAMILIAR-LOOKING LETTERS

Many letters of the Greek alphabet will be completely unfamiliar to you. But there are a few Greek letters that look and sound like letters you already know. Let's start your journey toward learning Greek by examining two familiar-looking letters.

The name of this letter is *tau* (rhymes with *now* and *cow*). Here's what it looks like in its uppercase form (on the left) and lowercase form (on the right).

T τ

This is the letter that was borrowed to become the letter *t* in the Latin alphabet.

Next, we have the letter *beta*. It looks and sounds like the letter *b*. Here it is in uppercase and lowercase forms.

B β

This is the letter that was borrowed to become the Latin letter *b*.

See? I told you that you would have a head start because some Greek letters would look and sound familiar. Congratulations—you now know two letters of the Greek alphabet!

LESSON FIVE

A GIMMICK FOR LEARNING

My goal here in the first part of this book is to teach you the letters of the Greek alphabet. You need to be able to recognize each letter and sound it out so that you can read and pronounce Greek words. In order to familiarize you with the Greek letters, I am going to use a special teaching technique...well, perhaps "gimmick" is a more accurate term.

Here's the gimmick: I will give you exercises in which we use Greek letters to spell out English words. Your challenge is to sound out these words, trying to figure out what the English word is supposed to be. If you sound out each Greek letter correctly, the English word should become clear.

As you work through the exercises in each lesson, you will gradually become familiar with most of the Greek alphabet. This gimmick—um, I mean, highly sophisticated teaching method—has its limitations and won't work for every letter, but it's a good way to get you started. Remember to have fun with it as you go along—you could even think of it as a game or a word puzzle. It's OK to have fun as you learn, so try to enjoy the learning process!

LESSON SIX

E ε

NAME: *epsilon*

SOUNDS LIKE: the *e* in *leg*

Our new letter for this lesson is called *epsilon*. It's an easy one to remember because it looks like the letter *e* in both upper and lowercase forms. It sounds like the *e* in *leg* or *peg*.

It's time now to start the gimmick in which I spell out English words with Greek letters and then you read them for practice. Here's an example to get you started. So far you know the letters *tau, beta,* and *epsilon*. I could use those letters to spell out an English word...can you figure out what it is?

βετ

If you guessed the word *bet*, you are correct! Right now, you only know enough Greek letters for me to be able to spell out one word. But as you learn more letters, I'll be able to spell out a greater variety of English words for the exercises. This will allow you to learn new letters while reviewing the letters you already know. So keep going, and remember to have fun as you go along.

LESSON SEVEN

NEW LETTER

Λ λ

NAME: *lambda*

SOUNDS LIKE: the *l* in *lake*

Our new letter for this lesson sounds like the *l* in *lake*. In its uppercase form it looks like an upside-down capital *v*. In its lowercase form it looks sort of like a lowercase *l* except with an extra "leg" sticking out toward the left.

In the following exercises, can you find the words *bet, let,* and *bell*? Remember to focus on how each word sounds, not necessarily on how it looks.

READING PRACTICE (ENGLISH WORDS)

1. βετ

2. λετ

3. βελ   βελλ

4. βελτ

5. τελ   τελλ

The answer to these exercises are on page 232.

LESSON EIGHT

NEW LETTER

NAME: *delta*

SOUNDS LIKE: the *d* in *dog*

Our new letter for this lesson is called *delta*. It sounds like the letter *d*. The uppercase form looks like a big triangle. The lowercase form looks sort of like a lowercase *d*, so it shouldn't be too hard to recognize.

In the exercises below, can you find the words *led*, *debt*, and *dell*?

READING PRACTICE (ENGLISH WORDS)

1. λεδ
2. δετ
3. δελ
4. βεδ
5. βελτ
6. τελ
7. λετ
8. βελ

Answers on page 232.

LESSON NINE

NEW LETTER

NAME: *phi* (pronounced *fie* or *fee*)
SOUNDS LIKE: the *f* in *food*

Our new letter for this lesson looks like a circle with a vertical slash through it.

In the exercises below, can you find the words *fell*, *left*, and *fed*?

READING PRACTICE (ENGLISH WORDS)

1. φελ
2. λεφτ
3. φεδ
4. δεφ
5. φελτ

6. βελ
7. λεδ
8. δετ
9. βελτ
10. βετ

Answers on page 232.

LESSON TEN

NEW LETTER

Ω ω

NAME: *omega*

SOUNDS LIKE: the *o* in *bone*

In its uppercase form, this letter looks a little like a horseshoe. The lowercase form looks sort of like a cursive letter *w*. *Omega* sounds like the *o* in *bone*, *tone*, and *cone*.

You may have seen the uppercase *omega* before in science class—it is the symbol for a unit of measurement called the *ohm*, which is used to measure resistance to electricity.

In the exercises below, can you find the words *boat*, *load*, and *loaf*?

READING PRACTICE (ENGLISH WORDS)

1. βωτ
2. λωδ
3. λωφ
4. φλωτ
5. φελω

6. φωτω
7. λεφτ
8. λεδ
9. φελτ
10. φεδ

Answers on page 232.

LESSON ELEVEN

NEW LETTER

N ν

NAME: *nu*

SOUNDS LIKE: the *n* in *noodle*

Our "nu" letter for this lesson looks very familiar in its uppercase form, but in its lowercase form it looks a bit like a lowercase *v*.

In the exercises below, can you find the words *phone*, *net*, and *tone*?

READING PRACTICE (ENGLISH WORDS)

1. φων
2. νετ
3. των
4. νωτ
5. λων
6. βων

7. φελω
8. λωφ
9. φεδ
10. βωτ
11. δετ
12. λωδ

Answers on page 232.

LESSON TWELVE

NEW LETTER

Σ σ ς

NAME: *sigma*

SOUNDS LIKE: the *s* in *soap*

Our new letter for this lesson is called *sigma*, and it sounds like the letter *s*.

There are three different forms of this letter. First, the uppercase form looks a little bit like a capital *e*, but with the middle line missing.

Then, there are two lowercase forms, each with a different purpose. One of them is used when the letter *sigma* comes at the beginning or middle of a word. It looks sort of like the letter *o* but with a little "arm" sticking out toward the right (that's the one in the middle). The other lowercase *sigma* (the one on the far right) is used when the letter *sigma* comes at the end of a word. That's why it's called *final sigma*. This one is easy to remember because it looks a lot like the letter *s*.

In the exercises below, can you find the words *sell*, *boats*, and *toast*?

READING PRACTICE (ENGLISH WORDS)

1. σελ
2. βωτς
3. τωστ
4. σλεδ
5. βωστ

6. σετ
7. βεστ
8. δως
9. νεστ
10. σνω

11. δεδ
12. λεφτ
13. των
14. φεδ
15. φωτω

Answers on page 232.

LESSON 13

K κ

NAME: *kappa*

SOUNDS LIKE: the *k* in *keep*

Our new letter for this lesson is called *kappa*. It's not difficult to remember at all because it looks and sounds like the letter *k* in both upper and lowercase forms.

In the exercises below, can you find the words *cone, soak,* and *neck?*

READING PRACTICE (ENGLISH WORDS)

1. κων	6. κωστ	11. φωτω
2. σωκ	7. δεκς	12. σλεδ
3. νεκ	8. νετς	13. νεστ
4. κωτ	9. τωστ	14. φων
5. κωδ	10. λωφ	15. σελ

Answers on page 232.

LESSON 14

Γ γ

NAME: *gamma*

SOUNDS LIKE: the *g* in *golf*

Our new letter for this lesson is called *gamma*. It sounds like the *g* in *golf.* In its uppercase form it looks like a capital *t*, but without the part that sticks out to the left. In its lowercase form it looks sort of like a cursive letter *y*. Depending on the font, the bottom part may look like a loop.

Here is something that you won't see too often, but you should at least be aware of. When the letter *gamma* comes immediately before certain Greek letters, it takes on a nasalized *n* sound, like the *n* in the word *angle*. If we see that in this book, I will point it out to you.

In the exercises below, can you find the words *goat, leg,* and *ghost?*

READING PRACTICE (ENGLISH WORDS)

1. γωτ	6. γωτς	11. νεστ
2. λεγ	7. λωγω	12. φεδ
3. γωστ	8. βεδ	13. βωστ
4. γες	9. σετ	14. φλωτ
5. εγ	10. δως	15. σνω

Answers on page 232.

14

LESSON 15

NEW LETTER

M μ

NAME: *mu* (pronounced *moo*)

SOUNDS LIKE: the *m* in *man*

Our new letter for this lesson is called *mu* (like the sound a cow makes). This Greek letter is the source of our letter *m*. Its uppercase form looks just like a capital *m*, and its lowercase form looks sort of like a cursive *u*, or perhaps an *m* that has been squished together.

In the exercises below, can you find the words *comb*, *melt*, and *dome*?

READING PRACTICE (ENGLISH WORDS)

1. κωμ
2. μελτ
3. δωμ
4. φωμ
5. μελτς

6. μωδ
7. μωστ
8. σμελ
9. λεγ
10. λωδ

11. γες
12. νεστ
13. κων
14. γωλ
15. φεδ

Answers on page 232.

15

LESSON 16

NEW LETTER

Π π

NAME: *pi* (pronounced *pie* or *pea*)
SOUNDS LIKE: the *p* in *party*

You may have seen the lowercase form of the letter *pi* in math class. In math, the letter *pi* stands for a special numerical value—the number of times that the diameter of a circle can fit around the outside of a circle. Here is the equation that shows the value of the letter *pi*.

$$\pi = \frac{C}{d}$$

In that equation, *C* stands for "circumference" and *d* stands for "diameter." When you divide the circumference by the diameter, you get a value of approximately 3.1416, which is what *pi* stands for.

In the exercises below, can you find the words *pet*, *soap*, and *pest*?

READING PRACTICE (ENGLISH WORDS)

1. πετ
2. σωπ
3. πεστ
4. κωπ
5. σλεδ

6. φλωτ
7. γωστ
8. νεστ
9. φωμ
10. φλεδ

11. μωστ
12. γωτς
13. νεκ
14. δεφ
15. λεγ

Answers on page 232.

LESSON 17

BREATHING MARKS

In the Greek alphabet, there is no letter that makes the sound of our letter *h*. In other words, no Greek letter can make the air-puffing sound at the beginning of words like *hop, have,* or *happy.*

Instead, Greek has special markings called *breathing marks.* There are two different breathing marks to learn: one is called a *smooth breathing* and the other is called a *rough breathing.* They look like little apostrophes, and they sit above a vowel.

Here is the letter *epsilon* twice, once with a smooth breathing mark over it and then again with a rough breathing mark over it.

Observe the smooth breathing mark (on the left) and notice that the bottom of it points to the left, like an apostrophe. Now observe the rough breathing mark (on the right) and notice that the bottom of it points to the right, like a *backwards* apostrophe.

Here is how the breathing marks work: the smooth breathing mark doesn't do anything. When you see a smooth breathing mark over a vowel, the pronunciation of that particular vowel does not change. But a rough breathing mark means that you should pronounce that vowel as if there were an *h* in front of it.

Now that we know how the breathing marks work, let's practice using them by spelling out the English words *elm* and *helm.* To spell out the word *elm,* let's use a smooth breathing, an *epsilon,* a *lambda,* and a *mu,* like this:

17

Since the smooth breathing doesn't change the sound of the vowel, the *epsilon* will sound like it always does, and the whole thing sounds like the English word *elm*.

Now let's spell out the English word *helm*. In order to do this, we will need a rough breathing to represent the *h* sound at the beginning of the word. So let's use a rough breathing (that's the one that points to the right), an *epsilon*, a *lambda*, and a *mu*, like this:

$$\dot{\epsilon}\lambda\mu$$

The rough breathing over the *epsilon* means that you must pronounce the *epsilon* as though there were an *h* in front of it. Then, the *lambda* and *mu* sound like they always do, and the whole thing sounds like the English word *helm*.

Whenever a Greek word starts with a vowel, that particular vowel *must* have either a smooth breathing mark or a rough breathing mark over it. It's mandatory! This means that whenever you see a Greek word that starts with a vowel, you must look carefully to see what kind of breathing mark is perched above the vowel. Then, you'll know what the beginning of the word sounds like. Sometimes you will see a Greek word that starts with a combination of two vowels—in that case, the breathing mark goes over the second vowel.

In the exercises below, can you find the words *hotel*, *elbow*, *oaks*, and *hoax*?

READING PRACTICE (ENGLISH WORDS)

1. ὠτελ	7. ἑλμ	13. φων
2. ἐλβω	8. ἑλμ	14. γες
3. ὠκς	9. ὠπ	15. νωτ
4. ὡκς	10. ἑδ	16. φωτω
5. ὡστ	11. πωπ	17. βων
6. ὡμ	12. γωστ	18. σωπς

Answers on page 232.

LESSON 18

NEW LETTER

NAME: *theta* (pronounced *THAY-tuh)*
SOUNDS LIKE: the *th* in *think*

The letter *theta* looks like an oval with a horizontal line in the middle. It sounds like the *th* in words such as *think, thought,* and *bath.*

In the exercises below, can you find the words *both, oath,* and *tenth?*

READING PRACTICE (ENGLISH WORDS)

1. βωθ
2. ὠθ
3. τενθ
4. δεπθ
5. δεθ
6. ἐδ

7. ἑλμ
8. ἐλβω
9. ὠκς
10. ὠστ
11. ὠμ
12. ἐλμ

13. ὠπ
14. ὠτελ
15. λωγω
16. φων
17. στεπ
18. τωστ

Answers on page 233.

LESSON 19

NAME: *xi* (pronounced *ksai* or *ksee*)
SOUNDS LIKE: the *x* in *box*

Our new letter for this lesson looks very different in its uppercase and lowercase forms. The uppercase version looks like three horizontal lines stacked on top of each other—but the lowercase version looks rather curly. If you practice writing out the lowercase version it will help you remember its shape.

The Greek letter *xi* functions just as the letter *x* does in English. Let's take a moment to think about the letter *x* and how it works. It's really like two letters in one—like the letter *k* and the letter *s* stuck together. For example, I could replace the *x* in an English word with the letters *k* and *s*, and it would sound the same. Here are a few examples of what I mean:

- box ➝ boks
- mix ➝ miks
- tax ➝ taks

In the same manner, I could take an English word spelled with *ks*, replace those two letters with an *x*, and it would sound the same.

- snacks ➝ snax
- backs ➝ bax
- larks ➝ larx

20

So you see, the letter *x* in English is a double letter in the sense that it contains the sounds of both a *k* and an *s*. This kind of consonant is called a *double consonant*.

Our new Greek letter for this lesson is a double consonant. Like the English letter *x*, the Greek letter *xi* contains both a *k* sound and an *s* sound. You might say that it is like a *kappa* and a *sigma* rolled into one. So if I wanted to spell out an English word that has a *k* and an *s* together, such as the word *soaks*, I could do it two ways. First, I could do it with a *kappa* and a *sigma*, like this...

σωκς

...or I could replace the *kappa* and *sigma* with the letter *xi*, like this, and it would sound the same:

σωξ

In the exercises below, can you find the words *oaks*, *necks*, and *hoax*? Don't be surprised if you find the same word spelled out two different ways.

READING PRACTICE (ENGLISH WORDS)

1. ὠκς
2. νεκς
3. ὠξ
4. νεξ
5. ὡκς
6. ὠθ

7. πωκς
8. πωξ
9. σωκς
10. σωξ
11. ὠπ
12. μελτς

13. πεστ
14. ἐλβω
15. φεδ
16. γωλ
17. νεοτς
18. βωθ

Answers on page 233.

LESSON 20

NEW LETTER

NAME: *psi* (pronounced *psai* or *psee*)
SOUNDS LIKE: the *ps* in *lips*

In the last lesson we observed that the letter *xi* is a double consonant because it is like a combination of the letters *kappa* and *sigma*. In this lesson I would like to teach you another double consonant: the letter *psi*.

The letter *psi* is like a combination of the letters *pi* and *sigma*. It sounds like the *ps* in words such as *lips*, *sips*, and *tips*. So if I wanted to spell out the word *soaps* with Greek letters, I could do it two ways—first, I could do it with a *pi* and a *sigma*, like this...

σωπς

...or I could do it with the letter *psi*, our new letter for this lesson:

σωψ

In the exercises below, can you find the words *hopes*, *mopes*, and *soaps*?

READING PRACTICE (ENGLISH WORDS)

1. ὠπς
2. ὠψ
3. μωπς
4. μωψ
5. σωπς
6. σωψ
7. ὠξ
8. βωθ
9. τενθ

22

10. δεθ

11. ὠθ

12. γωστ

13. δεπθ

14. νεξτ

15. ἐλμ

16. σωπ

17. κωπ

18. γεστ

Answers on page 233.

LESSON 21

NEW LETTER

NAME: *alpha*

SOUNDS LIKE: the *a* in *father*

Our new letter for this lesson is another familiar-looking one. It's called *alpha*, and it looks like the letter *a* in both its uppercase and lowercase forms.

In English, the letter *a* can be pronounced many ways. For example, it is pronounced differently in each of the following words:

- state
- cat
- gorilla
- father

But in ancient Greek, the letter *alpha* is much more consistent—it always sounds like the *a* in *father*. When the letter *a* has that kind of sound, it is sometimes referred to as "broad *a*." In English, we have a few words with that kind of vowel sound, but not too many. And most of the English words that have that particular vowel sound are actually spelled with an *o*, such as the words *dot* and *hot*.

In the exercises below, can you find the words *taco*, *dot*, and *hot*?

READING PRACTICE (ENGLISH WORDS)

1. τακω

2. δατ

3. ἁτ

4. λατ

5. πατ

6. τενθ

7. ὡψ

8. πωξ

9. σωψ

10. ὠθ

11. ἐλμ

12. σωκς

13. μωψ

14. βεγ

15. δεπθ

16. ὠξ

17. βωθ

18. νεξ

Answers on page 233.

LESSON 22

READING PRACTICE

In this lesson, let's take a break from learning new letters so you can practice reading the letters you already know. Each exercise has two words—can you figure them out without peeking at the answers?

READING PRACTICE (ENGLISH WORDS)

1. ἀτ τακω
2. βωθ γεστς
3. λεφτ λεγ
4. ὠξ φωτω
5. ὠτελ βεδ
6. βωτς φλωτ
7. ἑδ ὠμ
8. σνω μελτς
9. σελ φων
10. πετ γωτ
11. τενθ στεπ
12. ἐλβω βων
13. νεξτ σνω
14. βελ των
15. ὠκ βωτ

16. βεστ σωψ
17. τενθ τακω
18. ἀτ τωστ
19. δεδ φων
20. ὠμ δετ
21. φωμ σωπ
22. βωτ λωδ
23. γωτ σμελ
24. σνω σλεδ
25. λεγ βων
26. νεστ ἐγ
27. φων ὠμ
28. ἀτ πατ
29. σνω κων
30. ὠτελ λωγω

Answers on page 233.

LESSON 23

SOUNDS WE DON'T HAVE IN ENGLISH

Up to this point I have been spelling out English words with Greek letters. It's a gimmick that I am using to help you learn and read the letters of the Greek alphabet. So far, it has worked because I have carefully selected only certain Greek letters—letters representing sounds that exist both in English and in ancient Greek. Using only those specific letters, I have been able to spell out English words for you to practice with.

But now I need to teach you some Greek letters that represent sounds we don't have in English. This means that I can't easily spell out English words with them. So, over the next few lessons we will take a break from reading exercises as we examine letters with unfamiliar sounds.

If you want to pronounce these new letters correctly, you'll need to be ready and willing to experiment with making new and unfamiliar sounds. But don't be afraid to make a mistake or sound silly—experimentation is part of the learning process. Also, you should strive to listen carefully to the pronunciation recordings that accompany this book. They will help you to hear these sounds so you can copy them in your own pronunciation.

And, as I always say, remember to have fun as you go along. Think of it as an adventure, and don't be afraid to make a mistake or sound silly while you learn!

LESSON 24

P ρ

NAME: *rho* (rhymes with *snow*)
SOUNDS LIKE: a lightly rolled *r*

Our new letter for this lesson may generate some confusion for beginners. That's because it looks like the English letter *p* but sounds like the letter *r*. So at first, when you see it, you may be tempted to pronounce it like a *p*.

Why does it look like a *p* in the first place? To answer that question we must travel back in time. You see, the letter *rho* originally looked like this:

P

But then, when the Romans borrowed the letter *rho* for their alphabet, they added an extra "leg" to it, like this:

R

And that's the story of how we got the letter *r* (in its uppercase form, at least). So whenever you see the Greek letter *rho*, you can think of it as a letter *r* that is missing one "leg."

In ancient Greek, the *r* sound is lightly rolled, sort of like the way the letter *r* is pronounced in Spanish. This means that your tongue will flap lightly against the

27

roof of your mouth as you pronounce the letter *rho*. There's no need to make a heavy rolling sound—just keep it light.

By the way, when the letter *rho* comes at the beginning of a word, it will always have a rough breathing. It is the only consonant in the Greek alphabet that can take a breathing mark. Here's a demonstration, using a real ancient Greek word.

ῥῶψ

This word sounds something like *ropes*, but with a rolled *r* sound at the beginning. The rough breathing doesn't change the sound of the *rho* at the beginning—in other words, you don't need to try to incorporate an *h* sound into the sound of the *rho*.

LESSON 25

NEW LETTER

NAME: *chi* (pronounced *kai* or *key*)
SOUNDS LIKE: a light scraping sound, like the *ch* in *Bach* or *Chanukah*

Our new letter for this lesson represents a sound that may be unfamiliar to English speakers. It is a gentle scraping sound made in the back of the mouth. You may have heard this scraping sound if you have ever heard someone pronounce the name of the great composer J.S. Bach with an authentic German accent. Or, you may occasionally hear this sound if someone pronounces the name of the Jewish holiday *Hanukkah* (sometimes written as *Chanukah*) with an authentic Hebrew pronunciation. Anyway, be sure to listen to the audio recordings for this one!

LESSON 26

NEW LETTER

Z ζ

NAME: *zeta* (pronounced *ZAY-tuh*)
SOUNDS LIKE: like the *sd* in the word *wisdom*

Our new letter for this lesson is another double consonant. It's like a *z* sound and a *d* sound combined. You can get a grip on this letter by saying the word *wisdom* slowly and focusing on the transition between the *z* sound and the *d* sound.

The Greek language has been in constant use for well over 3,000 years! In that enormous span of time, the pronunciation of the Greek language has changed. Interestingly, Greek hasn't changed as much as other languages—but nevertheless there have been many variations at different times in history and in the many different places in which Greek was spoken. The letter *zeta* is one example of a letter that changed over time.

For this reason, if you continue to study Greek, a teacher may one day ask you to pronounce the letter *zeta* slightly differently than what I am telling you here. And that's OK—but as a beginner, it's a good idea to start out with a standard *zd* pronunciation, and then make those small adjustments in the future if needed.

LESSON 27

VOWEL LENGTH

At this point, you know all the letters of the Greek alphabet except for a few vowels. I have been deliberately saving these vowels for last because Greek vowels behave somewhat differently than they do in English. This means that as I teach you the Greek vowels, I also need to talk about some of the special characteristics that Greek vowels have.

The first characteristic of Greek vowels that I would like to talk about is vowel length. When I say length, I mean the duration of the vowel—that is, the actual time that you sustain the sound of the vowel when you pronounce it. As a simple exercise, say the word *potato* a few times. Notice that the letter *o* is found twice in this word:

p<u>o</u>tat<u>o</u>

As you pronounce the word *potato*, take a moment to focus on the *o* sounds. There is an *o* in the first syllable and then another *o* in the last syllable. Do they last the same amount of time?

I'm hoping that you noticed this: the *o* at the beginning of *potato* is very short, while the *o* at the end is much longer. The first *o* is so short that it doesn't really even have a full *o* sound. In fact, the first syllable goes by so quickly that it sounds something like a quick *puh*. The *o* at the end of *potato*, however, lasts noticeably longer. Therefore in the same word, the letter *o* has two completely different durations.

So here's the big idea I want you to take away from this lesson: a given vowel is not always pronounced with the same length or duration. Sometimes a vowel can be quick, but other times it can last longer. This is true both in English and in ancient Greek. Over the next few lessons, as we learn more vowels, we will also be examining how different vowel lengths can be expressed by Greek vowels.

30

LESSON 28

VOWEL LENGTH MAKES A BIG DIFFERENCE IN GREEK!

In ancient Greek, it's important to pronounce the vowels with the right length or duration. In ancient Greek, if you change the length of a vowel within a word, it can completely change the meaning of that word. This means that as a student of Greek, you should make an effort right from the very beginning to pronounce the various vowels with their correct lengths. It may take some extra effort in the short term, but in the long run it will save you lots of time and effort.

When you pronounce a Greek word with the correct vowel lengths, it gives that word a certain sound—and remembering that sound can help you remember how the word is spelled. This helps you to learn the relationship between how ancient Greek looks and the way it sounds. Also, in Greek you will sometimes encounter a certain word that is spelled almost the same as another word, and the only difference between the two words is the length of the vowel. By pronouncing each word with its correct vowel length, you will be more able to appreciate and remember the difference in spelling and meaning between similar words.

So here's my point: make an effort now, while you are a beginner, to get into the good habit of pronouncing Greek vowels with their correct lengths. A little extra effort now will pay you big dividends in the future!

LESSON 29

VOWEL PAIRS

In ancient Greek, certain vowels are always pronounced with a short duration while other vowels are always pronounced with a long duration. Then there are other vowels that can be either long or short.

Here's an example of a Greek vowel that is always long. It's a letter you already know—the letter *omega.*

The letter *omega* will always be long, and always should be pronounced with a long duration.

But what happens when you need to have an *o* sound in Greek with a short duration? There's a completely different letter for that. Let me introduce you to a vowel that you have not yet learned: the letter *omicron.* Here it is in both upper and lowercase forms.

O o

As you can see, the letter *omicron* looks just like the letter *o* in English. The letter *omicron* has the same vowel sound as the letter *omega,* but it's short. The letter *omicron* will always be short, and always should be pronounced with a short duration.

Since *omicron* and *omega* have the same vowel sound, the only difference is that *omicron* and *omega* have different durations. It's as if these two letters are partners, dividing up the work of making *o* sounds. One handles the short *o* sounds, while the other handles the long *o* sounds.

It can be helpful to imagine them as a pair of vowels, like this:

A good rule of thumb is that the long version of a vowel lasts twice as long as the short version of a vowel. So when you pronounce an *omega*, extend it out for double the time you would devote to an *omicron*.

Also, if you understand what the names of these letters mean in Greek, it can help you remember what function they have. The word *omicron* is comprised of two parts. The *o* at the beginning refers to an *o* sound. The rest of the word is the Greek word *mikron* which can mean *small* or *short*. We see this root word in English words such as *microscope* and *microchip*. Put *o* and *mikron* together and you get *omicron*, which literally means *short o*.

The word *omega* is also comprised of two parts. Again, the *o* at the beginning of the word refers to an *o* sound. The rest of the word is the Greek word *mega* which can mean *large* or *long*. We see this root word in English words such as *megabyte*, *megawatt*, and *megahertz*. Put *o* and *mega* together and you get *omega* which literally means *long o*.

In order to help you grasp the characteristics of each vowel and the relationships between vowels, I have created the following chart:

ANCIENT GREEK VOWEL LENGTHS

ALWAYS SHORT	O *omicron*
ALWAYS LONG	ω *omega*
COULD BE LONG OR SHORT	

This chart has three rows: one for vowels that are always short, one for vowels that are always long, and one for vowels that could be either long or short. Hopefully this chart can help you get a mental picture of the characteristics of the various vowels. Right now the chart only contains two vowels: *omicron*, which is always short, and *omega*, which is always long—but we will gradually add more vowels to the chart over the next few lessons.

LESSON 30

ANOTHER VOWEL PAIR

In the last lesson we learned that *omicron* and *omega* have a special relationship. They both have the same *o* sound, but *omicron* is always short while *omega* is always long. For this reason, we can think of them as a pair of vowels that share the responsibility of representing *o* sounds in ancient Greek.

In this lesson I would like to tell you about another similar vowel pair. Here is the short vowel of the pair—a vowel you already know:

The letter *epsilon* always will be short, and always should be pronounced with a short duration.

But there is another letter that has the same sound, except with a long duration. Let me introduce you to a vowel that you have not yet learned: the letter *eta* (pronounced *EIGHT-uh*). Here it is in both upper and lowercase forms.

$$H \quad \eta$$

In its uppercase form, the letter *eta* looks like a capital *h*. In its lowercase form it looks sort of like a lowercase *n* but with a longer right "leg." The letter *eta* has the same vowel sound as the letter *epsilon*, but with a long duration.

Just as with *omicron* and *omega*, you can picture *epsilon* and *eta* in your mind as a pair of vowels that work together:

$$\epsilon \longleftrightarrow \eta$$

SHORT   LONG

Again, a good rule of thumb is that the long version of a vowel lasts twice as long as the short version of a vowel. So when you pronounce an *eta*, extend it out for double the time you would devote to an *epsilon*.

As an experiment, try saying the word *leg*, but in a slow, extended way. Sustain the vowel sound, so it sounds something like *leeeeeeg*. The tone quality of that *e* sound is the tone quality of both the *epsilon* and the *eta*. The only difference between the two is the duration. So you see, these two letters work as a team with one covering the short sounds, and the other covering the long sounds.

Now that we know how these two vowels function, let's add them to our vowel length chart:

ANCIENT GREEK VOWEL LENGTHS

ALWAYS SHORT	ϵ *epsilon* O *omicron*
ALWAYS LONG	η *eta* ω *omega*
COULD BE LONG OR SHORT	

Now you only have a few vowels left—specifically, the ones that can be either long or short. And those are the vowels that we will begin to examine in the next lesson.

LESSON 31

VOWELS THAT CAN BE LONG OR SHORT

In Greek, certain vowels are always short, such as *epsilon* and *omicron*. Other vowels are always long, such as *eta* and *omega*. But some vowels do not have a predetermined length—they can be either short or long. Here's an example of one of those vowels that can be either short or long. It's a letter you already know:

$$\alpha$$

With some vowels such as *epsilon* or *omega*, you can tell what their length is just by looking at them. For example, you know in advance that the letter *epsilon* is always short, so it will be short every time you see it. But what about the letter *alpha*? When you see the letter *alpha*, how do you know whether it is long or short? The answer is that you can't tell what the length of an *alpha* is just by looking at it. For this reason, sometimes in dictionaries or textbooks you will see special markings that indicate whether a vowel is long or short. Here is what those special markings look like:

$$\text{—} \qquad \text{˘}$$

The mark on the left is called a *macron* (pronounced *MAKE-ron* or *MACK-ron*). It's used to indicate that a vowel is long. The curved mark on the right is called a *breve* (pronounced *breeve* or *brev*). It's used to indicate that a vowel is short. These marks sit above a vowel. Below, observe an *alpha* with a macron over it and then another *alpha* with a breve over it.

$$\bar{\alpha} \qquad \breve{\alpha}$$

The macron shows that the *alpha* on the left is a long *alpha*, while the breve shows that the *alpha* on the right is a short *alpha*. You'll never see these markings over

36

epsilon, eta, omicron, or *omega.* That's because their length never varies, so there is no need to indicate their length with any kind of marking.

If I were to mark every vowel with a macron or a breve, it could make the Greek text in this book look cluttered. For this reason, I will only mark a vowel when it is long. This means that for those particular vowels that can be either short or long, you should assume that they are short unless they have a macron. This way, the Greek text in this book can be a bit cleaner and easier to read.

Let's finish this lesson by adding *alpha* to our vowel length chart.

ANCIENT GREEK VOWEL LENGTHS

ALWAYS SHORT	ϵ epsilon	o omicron
ALWAYS LONG	η eta	ω omega
COULD BE LONG OR SHORT	α alpha	

Only two vowels left—you'll learn those in the next lesson.

LESSON 32

IOTA AND UPSILON

There are only two vowels left to learn: the letters *iota* and *upsilon*. Let's start with the letter *iota* (pronounced *eee-OH-tah* or *eye-OH-tah*). Here's what it looks like.

$$I \quad \iota$$

In both upper and lowercase forms, *iota* looks like the letter *i* (except without the dot). And, as you might guess, the letter *iota* is related to our letter *i*. *Iota* is one of those vowels that can be either long or short, so in some Greek books or dictionaries you might see it marked with a macron or breve, like this:

$$\bar{\iota} \qquad \breve{\iota}$$

Iota is pronounced like the *ee* in *meet* or *feet*. Try to pronounce a long *iota* about twice as long as you would pronounce a short *iota*.

Now here's the letter *upsilon* (pronounced *OOP-suh-lahn*):

$$Y \quad \upsilon$$

In its uppercase form, upsilon looks like an uppercase *y*. But in its lowercase form, it looks like the letter *u*. It's a long story, but the letter *upsilon* is related to the letter *u* (and also the letter *y*).

Upsilon is another one of those vowels that can be either short or long, so in some Greek books or dictionaries you might see it marked with a macron or breve, like this:

The letter *upsilon* is not pronounced exactly like the letter *u* in English. It's really a rounded vowel, meaning that you make your lips into a rounded shape when you pronounce it. Try saying the *ee* sound in words such as *feed* or *need*—and while sustaining that sound, form your lips into a rounded shape. The resulting sound may seem unusual to you—and if it does, you're probably doing it right!

Lets finish our study of vowels by adding these last two vowels to our vowel length chart.

ANCIENT GREEK VOWEL LENGTHS			
ALWAYS SHORT	ε *epsilon*	ο *omicron*	
ALWAYS LONG	η *eta*	ω *omega*	
COULD BE LONG OR SHORT	α *alpha*	ι *iota*	υ *upsilon*

As I mentioned before, please assume that every *alpha, iota,* and *upsilon* is short unless I mark it with a macron. And remember that *epsilon, eta, omicron,* and *omega* never need to have macrons or breves because their length never changes.

LESSON 33

DIPHTHONGS

The word *diphthong* (pronounced *DIFF-thong*) is a funny-sounding word, but it's an important word to know when learning ancient Greek. Speaking of Greek, this word comes to us from Greek roots. The first part of the word (the *di-* part) means *two.* The second part of the word (the *-phthong* part) means *voice* or *sound.* This is because a diphthong involves the blending of two vowel sounds.

The easiest way for me to explain how a diphthong works is by showing you an example. Say the following word slowly a few times and notice the movements your mouth makes as you say it.

boy

Your mouth starts out in a rounded shape as you pronounce the *o* sound, but your mouth changes shape as you glide into the *ee* sound of the letter *y.* Notice that as you glide from the *o* sound to the *ee* sound, your tongue moves upward, toward the roof of your mouth. And that gliding motion is really what a diphthong is—when you move between its *two sounds.*

Before you move to the next lesson, take some time to experiment with the diphthongs in each of these words (they are underlined).

- f<u>oi</u>l
- t<u>ie</u>
- cl<u>ou</u>d
- q<u>uee</u>n

Can you sense the movements that your lips and tongue make as you transition from the first vowel sound to the second vowel sound in each diphthong? When you've got the idea, proceed to the next lesson and we will begin to examine some Greek diphthongs.

LESSON 34

SOME GREEK DIPHTHONGS

In this lesson, let's learn some of the easier Greek diphthongs.

This first diphthong is made up of the letters *omicron* and *iota*. It sounds like the *oi* in English words such as *oil, foil,* and *toil.*

$$\text{οι}$$

This next diphthong is made up of the letters *alpha* and *iota*. It sounds like the English word *eye*. This kind of sound is found in many English words such as *mine, light,* and *sky.*

$$\text{αι}$$

Next we have a diphthong made up of the letters *alpha* and *upsilon*. It sounds like the *ow* in *how, now,* and *cow* (or what you say when you drop something on your toe).

$$\text{αυ}$$

In the exercises below, can you find the words *boy, sky, cloud,* and *fly?*

READING PRACTICE (ENGLISH WORDS)

1. βοι
2. σκαι
3. κλαυδ
4. φλαι

5. φοιλ
6. λαυδ
7. ται
8. σκαυτ

9. καυ
10. τοι
11. φαιν
12. δαυν

Answers on page 233.

LESSON 35

MORE GREEK DIPHTHONGS

The diphthongs in this lesson are a bit more challenging than the ones from the last lesson. Nevertheless, you should make an effort to master them because you will see them frequently.

This diphthong is made up of the letters *upsilon* and *iota*. It sounds like the vowel sound in the words *queen, sweet,* and *tweet.*

υι

This one is made up of the letters *omicron* and *upsilon*. This diphthong is kind of weird because it doesn't really have the sound of gliding from one vowel sound to another—instead, it sounds like the vowel sound in the words *moose, loose,* and *goose.*

ου

This one is a combination of the letters *epsilon* and *iota*. It's a long story (too long to tell here), but this particular combination of letters has gone through many changes throughout the history of the Greek language. Some Greek teachers pronounce it just like the letter *eta*. In this book, just for the sake of simplicity, I will pronounce it like the *ei* in *eight.*

ει

This last one is made up of the letters *epsilon* and *upsilon*. It sounds like the *e* in *leg* followed quickly by the *oo* in *boot*. We don't have this sound in English, so it won't be included in the pronunciation exercises. Instead, I'll remind you of what it sounds like when we see it.

ευ

In the following exercises, can you find the words *queen, goose, fate,* and *sweet*?

1. κυιν

2. γους

3. φειτ

4. συιτ

5. λειτ

6. τυιτ

7. λουμ

8. σκειτ

9. συιπ

10. τουλ

11. φαιν

12. καυ

13. ται

14. σκαι

15. δαυν

16. βοι

17. κλαυδ

18. τοι

19. φοιλ

20. σκουτ

21. φλαι

Answers on page 233.

LESSON 36

DIPHTHONGS AND BREATHING MARKS

You already know that when a Greek word begins with a vowel, that vowel must have a breathing mark over it. This rule also applies to diphthongs. But there is one small difference with diphthongs—when a diphthong begins a Greek word, the breathing mark sits above the second vowel in the diphthong, not the first.

For example, if a Greek word were to begin with the diphthong αι, the beginning of the word would look like one of the two examples below.

Remember that the two vowels in a diphthong are working together as one unit. So even though the breathing mark sits above the second vowel (the *iota*), it affects the sound of the beginning of the diphthong, not just the second letter. Therefore the example on the left sounds something like the word *eye*, while the example on the right sounds something like the word *high*.

In the following exercises, can you find the words *hoist*, *week*, *high*, and *house*?

READING PRACTICE (ENGLISH WORDS)

1. οἰστ	11. αὐλ	21. σκουτ
2. υἰκ	12. φειτ	22. ται
3. αἱ	13. φλαι	23. καυ
4. αὐς	14. κυιν	24. λαυδ
5. οὐπ	15. βοι	25. τουλ
6. αὐτ	16. συιτ	26. λειτ
7. αὑ	17. τοι	27. κλαυδ
8. αἰς	18. γους	28. φαιν
9. υἰπ	19. συιπ	29. φοιλ
10. αἰτ	20. λουμ	30. τυιτ

Answers on page 234.

44

LESSON 37

Congratulations! You now have a basic familiarity with the Greek alphabet and you're ready to start reading real Greek words. But before we do that, I would like for you to take a moment to review all that you have learned. As you go forward, try to keep the following items in mind.

1. The Latin alphabet (used by English speakers) was adapted from the Greek alphabet. For this reason, some Greek letters will look familiar to English speakers, especially capital letters.

2. Sometimes an uppercase Greek letter looks the same as its lowercase form, only bigger. Other times the uppercase form will look rather different.

3. It's a good idea to write out Greek letters and words for practice. If you practice writing Greek on a regular basis, you will learn the language faster and better.

4. Breathing marks are little marks that go along with the vowels or diphthongs that begin a Greek word. They indicate whether or not the vowel or diphthong should be pronounced with an *h* sound in front of it.

5. Whenever a Greek word begins with a vowel or diphthong, that vowel or diphthong *must* have a breathing mark over it.

6. The letter *xi* is a double consonant, as if it were a combination of a *kappa* and a *sigma*.

7. The letter *psi* is a double consonant, as if it were a combination of a *pi* and a *sigma*.

8. Greek vowels have different lengths, or durations. *Epsilon* and *omicron* are always short. *Eta* and *omega* are always long. *Alpha*, *iota*, and *upsilon* can be either long or short.

9. A macron is a small horizontal line that sits above a vowel. It indicates that a vowel is long.

10. A breve is a curved line that sits above a vowel. It indicates that a vowel is short.

11. In this book, *alpha, iota,* and *upsilon* will be short unless they are marked with a macron.

12. The vowels *epsilon* and *eta* both have the same vowel sound, but different durations. They can be thought of as a pair of vowels that work together, with *epsilon* representing the short sounds and *eta* representing the long sounds.

13. The vowels *omicron* and *omega* both have the same vowel sound, but different durations. They can be thought of as a pair of vowels that work together, with *omicron* representing the short sounds and *omega* representing the long sounds.

14. A diphthong is a blending of two vowels. Common diphthongs that you will see in this book are αι *(mine, fine, pine),* οι *(boy, foil, oil),* ου *(moose, loose, goose),* υι *(queen, sweet, tweet),* αυ *(how, now, cow).* It's a long story, but in this book we will pronounce ει like the vowel sound in *eight.*

15. When a diphthong has a breathing mark over it, the breathing mark sits above the second vowel of the diphthong. The breathing mark affects the sound of the beginning of the entire diphthong, not the beginning of the sound of the second letter.

16. The uppercase forms of *gamma* (Γ), *delta* (Δ), *eta* (H), *lambda* (Λ), *xi* (Ξ), *sigma* (Σ), *upsilon* (Υ), and *omega* (Ω) should be given special attention because they don't look like their lowercase forms and they don't look like any letters from the Latin alphabet.

LESSON 38

ACCENT MARKINGS

In some languages such as English, each word has its own special pattern of stressed and unstressed syllables. For example, in the word *potato*, the second syllable receives the stress or emphasis. This pattern of stressed and unstressed syllables is part of what distinguishes one word from another and makes them recognizable. Other languages, such as French, do not have stressed and unstressed syllables—every syllable is supposed to have the same level of emphasis.

Ancient Greek is...well, it's a long story. During the Classical period, instead of a stress-based accent, Greek was spoken with a pitch accent. This means that the pitch of the speaker's voice would go up on certain syllables and down on other syllables.

Long ago, a fellow named Aristophanes of Byzantium was the chief librarian at the library of Alexandria, Egypt. He lived from about 257 BC to about 180 BC. He invented special markings to indicate when the pitch of the voice was supposed to go up and down. Here's what they look like, each positioned over the letter *alpha*:

The one on the far left is called an *acute* accent. It points upward, indicating that the pitch of the speaker's voice was supposed to go up. The one in the middle is called a *grave* (pronounced *grahv*) accent. It points down, indicating that the pitch of the speaker's voice was supposed to go down. The one on the far right is called a *circumflex*. It indicated that the pitch of the voice was supposed to go up and down on the same syllable. The circumflex can be written like an upside-down letter *u*, or it can be written like a wavy line called a *tilde*. It really depends on the font or typeface that is being used to print a particular Greek text. But

47

either way, it's the same thing, so don't let it confuse you. In this book, I will use the kind of circumflex that looks like an upside-down *u*.

But the story doesn't end there—over the centuries, the pronunciation of the Greek language gradually changed from a pitch accent to a stress-based accent. And today, when ancient Greek is taught, it is taught with a stress accent. But, strangely, the accent marks used for printed Greek are the ones that were designed to show pitch accent. See? I told you it was a long story.

So here's what all this means for you as a beginner: when you are reading a Greek word, just put the stress on whatever syllable has any kind of accent over it. Don't worry about pitch accents. As long as you put the emphasis on the right syllable, you'll be fine.

Let's practice this a bit with a new Greek word—the word for *farmer*.

γεωργός

This word sounds something like *geh-orr-GOHS*. The stress, or emphasis, is on the final syllable, therefore the word has an accent mark over that particular syllable. In this manner, accent marks in Greek show you how a word is supposed to be pronounced. For example, when you see γεωργός, you know that it is not pronounced with the emphasis on the first syllable, like *GEH-orr-gohs*, or with the emphasis on the second syllable, like *geh-ORR-gohs*. So as you read Greek, pay attention to where the accents are in a Greek word and they will take you a long way toward correct pronunciation.

By the way, like many Greek words, the word γεωργός is a combination of smaller words. The first part of the word means *earth* and the second part means *work*. The basic idea is that it means someone who works the earth, therefore a farmer. This Greek word is the source of English names such as *George, Georgina,* and *Georgia.* As we go through this book, we will discover many more English words which are derived from Greek roots.

LESSON 39

ACCENTS AND BREATHING MARKS ON THE SAME LETTER

As you may have noticed by now, ancient Greek has lots of different markings that can sit above various letters. Sometimes there will even be more than one marking parked above one letter. This can be visually confusing for the beginner.

Here's an example of what I mean: sometimes, at the beginning of a word, you will see both a breathing mark and an accent next to each other, over the same vowel. Here's the Greek word for *chair* as an example.

ἕδρα

This word sounds like *HEH-dra*. It starts out with the letter *epsilon* and a rough breathing—but also, since the stress is on the first syllable, there is an accent mark there too. Notice that the breathing mark and the accent are crammed in together over the *epsilon*. I'll enlarge the first letter of the word and label the different parts so you can more easily see what is going on:

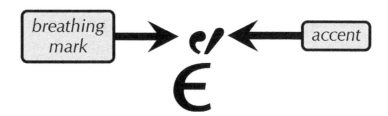

Don't be confused by the fact that these two markings are crammed together— each individual mark is still doing what it usually does. The rough breathing mark tells you to make an *h* sound, and the accent mark tells you to put the stress on that syllable.

The only place you will see this is at the beginning of a word, because that's the only part of a Greek word that can have a breathing mark. So when you see both a breathing mark and an accent at the beginning of a word, look carefully so you can figure out how the beginning of the word is supposed to sound.

LESSON 40

ARTICLES

Articles are words such as *the, a,* and *an.* Let's take a look at some examples:

The man
The woman
A chair
An apple

A noun is a person, place, or thing. In each of the examples above, we used an article to introduce each noun.

Let's talk about the difference between the word *the* and the word *a/an.* The word *the* is called the *definite article.* Why? Because when you use it, you are referring to a definite thing. Here's an example:

Please go into the garage and get the broom.

When you make a statement like this, it is clear that you are referring not to just any broom—instead, you have a specific broom in mind, and you want someone to go and get it! You are referring to a definite thing, therefore *the* is a definite article.

In English, the words *a* and *an* are called *indefinite articles.* Why? Because they don't refer to any specific item. Instead, they just refer to any item that fits the description. Here's an example:

Please go into the garage and get a broom.

When you make a statement like this, you are not referring to any specific broom. In fact, there may be several brooms in the garage, and you are just asking someone to go and pick one—any broom will do. The thing you are asking for is indefinite, therefore *a* and *an* are indefinite articles.

LESSON 41

ARTICLES IN GREEK

In the last lesson, we learned about the difference between definite and indefinite articles. Now let's learn how to express those same things in ancient Greek.

Articles introduce nouns, so we need a noun to work with. Fortunately, you already know the Greek word for *farmer*:

γεωργός

Now let's learn the word for *the*, which is called the *definite article*. Here it is:

ὁ

This short word consists only of the letter *omicron* and a rough breathing. Therefore it will sound like the *ho* in the word *hoax*. Some Greek teachers don't like to call this word the definite article, but for the sake of simplicity, that's what I'll call it in this book.

Now let's put the definite article and the noun together:

ὁ γεωργός *(the farmer)*

Now you know how to say *the farmer*. But what if you don't want to refer to a specific farmer? What if you just want to say *a farmer*?

It's kind of a long story, but ancient Greek doesn't have an indefinite article in the same way that English does. Instead, in ancient Greek, if you want to say *a farmer* you would just put the noun by itself, without an article to introduce it, like this:

γεωργός

So, when you see a noun and there is no article in front of it, you can translate it into English with an indefinite article. Therefore the example above could be translated as *a farmer*.

There is much more to know about Greek articles and how they are used. The rules I described above are just broad generalizations—oversimplifications, really, to help you get started. As you gain more experience translating Greek, you will learn more about the nuances of Greek articles. But for now, keep these simple rules in mind as you work through the exercises.

LESSON 42

GENDER

In ancient Greek, each noun is classified as having a certain gender. A noun can be either masculine, feminine, or neuter (the word *neuter* means neither masculine nor feminine). Every Greek noun has a gender—not just nouns that refer to people or animals. Even nouns that refer to everyday objects such as boats, tables, mountains, or buildings have gender. So, whenever you learn a new Greek noun, you must make an effort to remember what gender that particular noun is.

In this book I will only teach you the masculine gender. This is for one simple reason—because it allows me to give you the easiest possible introduction to ancient Greek. Ancient Greek can be complicated, especially for beginners, but the masculine nouns that I will teach you in this book are the least complicated way for me to introduce you to the way Greek nouns work. In the future, when you learn about feminine and neuter nouns, you'll have an easier time with them because you'll already know some good, basic concepts about Greek nouns and you won't be starting from scratch.

You already know one masculine noun, and that's the word γεωργός. Soon, you'll learn more masculine nouns and we will be able to form simple sentences. So turn the page and get ready for your first lesson that includes real translation exercises!

LESSON 43

NEW WORD   διδάσκαλος

MEANING   *teacher*

PRONUNCIATION TIP: The word διδάσκαλος has four syllables. The accent mark is over the second syllable, so it sounds like *di-DAHS-ka-lohs*.

When you first learned the word γεωργός, I mentioned that we have related English words such as *George, Georgina,* and *Georgia*. We also have several English words related to our new word for this lesson. For example, the English word *didactic* means *instructive* or *teaching-oriented*.

This lesson is a special one because it contains the first set of Greek exercises that you must translate into English. As you translate, remember what you learned about articles: translate the definite article ὁ as *the*. If a noun is not introduced by ὁ then you can translate it into English with the indefinite article *a* or *an*.

EXERCISES

1. ὁ διδάσκαλος

2. διδάσκαλος

3. ὁ γεωργός

4. γεωργός

Answers on page 234.

LESSON 44

PRONOUNS

A pronoun is a word that can take the place of a noun. Pronouns are words like *he, she, it, I, we, you,* and *they.* We often use pronouns when we have already used a certain noun once and do not want to say that same noun again. Observe this example:

> Susanne is wearing a blue dress. <u>Susanne</u> bought the dress last week.

Instead of repeating the word *Susanne* in the second sentence, we can replace it with a pronoun, like this:

> Susanne is wearing a blue dress. <u>She</u> bought the dress last week.

In this way, pronouns can help us avoid repeating the names of the things or people we are talking about.

In each of the following exercises, try to identify the pronoun. And, if the pronoun is taking the place of another word, identify that word also.

EXERCISES

1. Alfred's room is a mess because he never cleans up.
2. Jeff does not like going to the locker room because it is too smelly.
3. She already went to school.
4. The kids want to come inside because they are cold.
5. The teacher told Johnny to stop, but he didn't listen.
6. We are going to the beach.
7. They are not going to the party.
8. You are sitting in the wrong chair.
9. The rabbit was scared, so it ran away.
10. Don't disturb the children; they are asleep.

Answers on page 234.

LESSON 45

NEW WORD   εἰμί

MEANING   *I am*

PRONUNCIATION TIP: In this book we will pronounce the ει diphthong like the *ei* in the word *eight*. The word εἰμί starts with a smooth breathing and has its accent on the second syllable, so it sounds like *ei-MEE*.

In English, it takes two words to say *I am*. In Greek, it takes only one: εἰμί. This is because every Greek verb has a pronoun included in it. For example, the word εἰμί includes both the pronoun *I* and the verb *am*, all in one word.

Now that you know how to say *I am* in ancient Greek, we can make complete sentences like these:

- εἰμὶ ὁ διδάσκαλος. *(I am the teacher.)*
- εἰμὶ διδάσκαλος. *(I am a teacher.)*

Can you translate these exercises into English? The first word of each sentence will not be capitalized unless it is the name of a person.

EXERCISES

1. εἰμί.

2. εἰμὶ διδάσκαλος.

3. εἰμὶ ὁ διδάσκαλος.

4. εἰμὶ γεωργός.

5. εἰμὶ ὁ γεωργός.

Answers on page 234.

LESSON 46

SOME GREEK NAMES

It's time to learn a few Greek names so that we can make more interesting sentences. Just as in English, a person's name in Greek will start with a capital letter.

Let's start with a famous one: the name *Alexander*. This was the name of Alexander the Great who conquered the Persian Empire in the fourth century BC. Here's how it looks in ancient Greek:

Ἀλέξανδρος

The first letter of this name is an uppercase *alpha*. It has a smooth breathing placed at the upper left side of the *alpha*. Since uppercase letters are tall, the breathing mark gets parked slightly to the left of the letter instead of directly above it. This word has four syllables just like the English word Alexander—but there is a big difference to be aware of. In English, we put the stress on the next-to-last syllable, like this: *a-lek-SANN-durr*. But in ancient Greek, this word has the stress on the second syllable (notice the accent over the letter *epsilon*). Therefore it sounds something like *ah-LEK-sahn-drohss*.

This next name is from the famous epic poem known as the *Odyssey* by the blind poet Homer. In the poem, Telemachus is the son of the crafty Odysseus and his faithful wife Penelope. Here's how this word looks:

Τηλέμαχος

This name has four syllables with the stress on the second syllable, so it sounds something like *teh-LEH-mah-chos*. Remember that the letter *eta* is a long syllable and that the letter *chi* represents a light, gentle scraping sound.

Here's another name from Greek mythology: Cadmus. Here's how it looks:

Κάδμος

The first letter of this name is an uppercase *kappa*. This word has two syllables, and the stress is on the first syllable, so it sounds something like *KAHD-mohss*. According to Greek myth, Cadmus was the king of a famous Greek city called Thebes. As the story goes, he was responsible for introducing the Phoenician alphabet to the Greeks, who borrowed it and used it to form the Greek alphabet. So if you think the Greek alphabet is difficult, don't blame me—blame Cadmus!

Generally speaking, Greek names that end with ‑ος come into English with the ending *-us*. That's because the ancient Romans had to change the spellings of Greek words from the Greek alphabet into the Roman alphabet—so the ‑ος at the end of a Greek word was spelled as *-us* in the Latin alphabet. Then, that Latin spelling is the spelling that would later find its way into English. This is one of several reasons why Anglicized versions of Greek names sometimes differ from their original Greek forms.

EXERCISES

1. εἰμί.

2. εἰμὶ Ἀλέξανδρος.

3. εἰμὶ Κάδμος.

4. εἰμὶ Τηλέμαχος.

5. εἰμὶ γεωργός.

6. εἰμὶ ὁ γεωργός.

7. εἰμὶ διδάσκαλος.

8. εἰμὶ ὁ διδάσκαλος.

Answers on page 234.

LESSON 47

THE DEFINITE ARTICLE WITH NAMES

In ancient Greek, you will often see the definite article used with a person's name. For example, you might see this:

ὁ Ἀλέξανδρος

Whenever you see a name with a definite article in front of it, do not translate the definite article. Just ignore it. For example, if you see ὁ Ἀλέξανδρος you would translate it into English simply as *Alexander*, not as *the Alexander*.

EXERCISES

1. εἰμί.

2. εἰμὶ ὁ Ἀλέξανδρος.

3. εἰμὶ Κάδμος.

4. εἰμὶ ὁ γεωργός.

5. εἰμὶ Τηλέμαχος.

6. εἰμὶ διδάσκαλος.

7. εἰμὶ ὁ Κάδμος.

8. εἰμὶ γεωργός.

9. εἰμὶ ὁ διδάσκαλος.

10. εἰμὶ ὁ Τηλέμαχος.

Answers on page 234.

LESSON 48

YOU DON'T NEED TO KNOW EVERYTHING ABOUT ACCENTS

Most ancient Greek textbooks cover all the complicated rules about accents right at the very beginning of the book. This can overwhelm and frustrate the beginning Greek student. But here is the reality: *As a beginner, you do not need to know all the accent rules and terms right now.* For beginners, there is so much new information to absorb—and accent rules are things that you can learn over time as you gain more experience working with Greek.

Instead of memorizing a list of rules that you don't really understand, a better way to spend your time at this stage is to listen to recordings of ancient Greek (that's the reason why I have created so many recordings to go along with this book). If you, as a beginner, listen repeatedly to simple pronunciation recordings, you will begin to hear and notice the different sound patterns of the Greek language. Then, the various rules of Greek accents will make more sense to you because you'll already know how it sounds when those rules are applied to actual Greek sentences. In other words, you can learn the sounds first, then learn the rules that explain those sounds. It's the same way in music—even if you don't know how to read written music, you can still learn a song by listening to it.

It is important for all language students (and teachers, too) to remember that languages start out as spoken sounds, not as written words. Ancient peoples spoke their languages long before they found ways to write them down. So as you study Greek, don't just think about how Greek looks when written—also think about how the language *sounds*. If you listen to recordings of ancient Greek daily and try to say something in Greek daily, you will learn faster and better—so incorporate these practices into your daily study habits, and don't miss out on all the benefits they have to offer.

LESSON 49

BASIC ACCENT RULES

In ancient Greek there are certain rules that govern the placement of accents. According to these rules, every Greek word (with a few exceptions) should have an accent—but accents are only allowed to go on the last three syllables of a word. Also, each kind of accent can only go on certain syllables. One kind of accent can only go on the last syllable of a word. Another kind of accent can only go on the last or next-to-last syllable. And yet another kind can go on any of the last three syllables of a word. Therefore as part of your study of Greek accents, you must know how to count syllables backward from the end of a word and figure out how far each syllable is from the end.

Let's practice the syllable-counting method I just described using the familiar word γεωργός. First, let's split it up into its individual syllables.

γε   ωρ   γός

Now, starting at the end of the word, let's count backward and number each syllable.

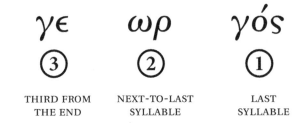

γε   ωρ   γός

③   ②   ①

THIRD FROM   NEXT-TO-LAST   LAST
THE END   SYLLABLE   SYLLABLE

Now we have identified which syllable is last, next-to-last, and third from the end. This counting process is a fundamental skill for working with Greek accents.

As I mentioned a moment ago, accents can only go on the last three syllables of a Greek word. You already know several Greek words that have four syllables. If you examine them, you'll find that the fourth syllable from the end never has the accent. Here's an example of what I mean, using the word διδάσκαλος as an example:

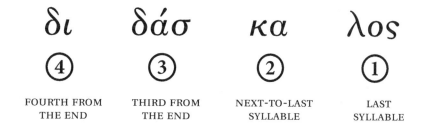

δι	δάσ	κα	λος
④	③	②	①
FOURTH FROM THE END	THIRD FROM THE END	NEXT-TO-LAST SYLLABLE	LAST SYLLABLE

See what I mean? Accents can only go on the last three syllables. Therefore, since the δι syllable in διδάσκαλος is the fourth from the end, it can't have an accent. You'll find this same thing is true for the other four-syllable words you know, which are Τηλέμαχος and Ἀλέξανδρος.

And since we are on the subject of accents, let's finish up this lesson with a quick review of the names of the different kinds of accents. In the chart below, each kind of accent is displayed over the letter *alpha*.

ANCIENT GREEK ACCENTS

ACUTE	ά
GRAVE	ὰ
CIRCUMFLEX	ᾶ or ᾶ

LESSON 50

IN GREEK, WORD ORDER IS FLEXIBLE

In ancient Greek, the order of words in a sentence is more flexible than in English. Let's say that you see this sentence in Greek:

> εἰμὶ γεωργός.

A word-for-word translation of that sentence would be *I am (a) farmer.* To an English speaker, that would seem like a normal word order because the Greek words are in the same order as they would be if the sentence were in English. But what if we change the order a bit?

> γεωργός εἰμι.

A word-for-word translation of that sentence would be *(A) farmer I am.* A native English speaker would view that word order as unusual, but would still understand what the sentence is saying. Even though this kind of wording is not used in everyday conversation, a native speaker has probably heard that kind of word order many times in old songs or poems. Therefore to an English speaker, *I am a farmer* would seem like the normal, expected word order for that sentence, while *A farmer I am* would seem like an unusual word order, although still perfectly understandable.

But in ancient Greek, neither of the sentences shown above would seem unusual. To an ancient Greek person, εἰμὶ γεωργός and γεωργός εἰμι would both have sounded normal, and both would have meant the same thing. So this means that as you read Greek you will have to get used to seeing the words in a different order than you might expect in an English sentence. This will become easier with practice.

Finally, remember that no matter what the word order is in a Greek sentence, you should still translate it into English with a natural-sounding English word order.

EXERCISES

1. εἰμί.

2. εἰμὶ γεωργός.

3. γεωργός εἰμι.

4. εἰμὶ διδάσκαλος.

5. ὁ διδάσκαλός εἰμι.

6. ὁ γεωργός εἰμι.

7. εἰμὶ ὁ διδάσκαλος.

8. εἰμὶ Τηλέμαχος.

9. Κάδμος εἰμί.

10. Ἀλέξανδρός εἰμι.

Answers on page 234.

LESSON 51

ENCLITICS

When you are working with Greek accents, you must count backward from the end of the word in order to identify which syllable is last, which one is next-to-last, and so on and so forth. At this stage you are only a beginner at ancient Greek, so you don't need to know everything there is to know about accents. However there is one additional thing I would like to mention before we move on from the topic of accents. In this lesson I'd like to tell you about a special kind of Greek word called an *enclitic*.

An enclitic is a word that wants to give away its accent to the word that comes before it. You already know one enclitic, and that is the word εἰμί. On its own, the word εἰμί has an accent on its final syllable, like this:

εἰμί

But if another word comes before εἰμί, something special happens: εἰμί gives away its accent to the previous word, like this:

γεωργός εἰμι

Notice that in that particular example, εἰμί no longer has an accent on its second syllable.

Enclitics behave in this way because they join with the previous word for the purpose of counting syllables. In the example above, the word εἰμί has joined itself to the word γεωργός to create a larger syllable-counting unit that is made up of two words. There will still be a space between words—the two words don't actually join together into one word. But they do form one unit as far as the counting of syllables. So with γεωργός and εἰμί joined together into one syllable-counting unit, here is how it would look if you numbered the syllables:

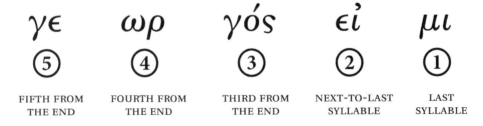

γε	ωρ	γός	εἰ	μι
⑤	④	③	②	①
FIFTH FROM THE END	FOURTH FROM THE END	THIRD FROM THE END	NEXT-TO-LAST SYLLABLE	LAST SYLLABLE

Now that these words have joined their syllables into one big counting unit, the syllables must be identified differently. The syllable γός is now considered to be the third-to-last syllable. The syllable ωρ is now the fourth syllable from the end and γε is now the fifth syllable from the end.

My goal in this lesson has been to give you an extremely basic introduction to enclitics. The rules for enclitics can be a bit complicated, and you don't need to know them all right now. Just be aware that depending on the characteristics of the previous word, an enclitic can...

1. Keep its accent

2. Give away its accent to the previous word

3. Cause the previous word to have two accents

As item #3 mentions, under the right circumstances, a word can have two accents. And when this happens, one of the accents can be more than three syllables away from the end of the syllable-counting unit—so don't let that surprise you.

LESSON 52

HOW TO GET THE MOST OUT OF LISTENING TO RECORDINGS

In order to help you learn, I have provided many audio recordings to go along with this book. These recordings will help you learn better and faster. But did you know that there is more than one way to listen to a language recording? Here are some of the different strategies you can use as you listen.

- **Focus on translation:** As you listen to a Greek exercise, try to mentally translate it into English.

- **Focus on Spelling:** As you listen to an exercise, try to visualize how each word would be spelled (Hmmm…was that word spelled with an *omega* or an *omicron*?).

- **Focus on Sound and Pronunciation:** Try to repeat an exercise correctly with all the proper accents, vowel lengths, etc.

- **Focus on Meaning:** As you listen to a recording of a Greek sentence, don't mentally translate it into English. In other words, listen to the Greek words and try to picture in your mind what is happening without using English as an intermediate step to understanding what is being said.

So you see, there are many ways to listen, each of them educational and beneficial. And the more time you devote to listening, the more quickly you will understand the relationship between the way Greek looks in written form and the way it sounds. Don't miss out on the enormous benefits that listening can give you!

LESSON 53

NEW WORD   ἰᾱτρός

MEANING   *doctor*

PRONUNCIATION TIP: Notice that both the *iota* and the *alpha* at the beginning of this word have macrons, indicating that they are long vowels. This word starts with a smooth breathing, therefore it sounds like *eee-ah-TROHSS*.

Our new word for this lesson is related to the English word *pediatrician*. A pediatrician is a doctor who specializes in helping children. The *ped-* at the beginning of the word comes from the Greek word for *child*. The *-iatr-* part of the word is from ἰᾱτρός. So literally, the word *pediatrician* means *child-doctor*.

EXERCISES

1. εἰμὶ ἰᾱτρός.

2. ὁ ἰᾱτρός εἰμι.

3. γεωργός εἰμι.

4. εἰμὶ ὁ γεωργός.

5. εἰμὶ Ἀλέξανδρος.

6. εἰμὶ ὁ διδάσκαλος.

7. ὁ Τηλέμαχός εἰμι.

8. εἰμὶ Κάδμος.

9. Τηλέμαχός εἰμι.

10. εἰμὶ ὁ Ἀλέξανδρος.

Answers on page 234.

LESSON 54

NEW WORD   φιλόσοφος

MEANING   *philosopher*

Like many Greek words, our new word for this lesson is a combination of two smaller words. The φιλο- part of the word is from a Greek verb that means *to love*. The -σοφος part is from the Greek noun *sophia* which means *wisdom*. So our new word for this lesson literally means *wisdom-lover*.

EXERCISES

1. φιλόσοφός εἰμι.

2. ὁ φιλόσοφός εἰμι.

3. εἰμὶ φιλόσοφος.

4. εἰμὶ ὁ φιλόσοφος.

5. γεωργός εἰμι.

6. Τηλέμαχός εἰμι.

7. ὁ διδάσκαλός εἰμι.

8. Κάδμος εἰμί.

9. Ἀλέξανδρός εἰμι.

10. εἰμὶ ὁ ἰᾱτρός.

Answers on page 234.

LESSON 55

SUBJECTS

A noun is a person, place, or thing. The subject of a sentence is the noun that is doing the action in the sentence. In the Greek sentences you have seen so far, the subject of the sentence has always been *I*, but soon you will learn to read more complex Greek sentences.

Just for practice, see if you can identify the subject of each of the following sentences.

EXERCISES

1. I am.
2. You are.
3. She is tall.
4. On Tuesdays and Thursdays, Fred likes to go jogging.
5. Chicago is a big city.
6. The children have ice cream cones.
7. The car has a flat tire.
8. My oatmeal is too hot.
9. Switzerland is a beautiful country.
10. In the winter, Grandfather always wears his old brown coat.

Answers on page 235.

LESSON 56

VERBS

In the last lesson, you learned to recognize the subject of a sentence. Now let's talk about verbs. Verbs are words that tell us what the subject of a sentence is doing. Verbs can be action words such as *dance, shout, walk, talk,* or *write.* Or, they can be verbs of being or existing such as *is, are, was, were,* and *will be.* Verbs of being are also called *linking verbs.*

Just for practice, see if you can identify the subject and verb of each of the following sentences.

EXERCISES

1. She walks to school every day.
2. My car is dirty.
3. I see a quarter on the ground.
4. Yesterday he bought a trumpet.
5. Sam loves chocolate milk.
6. They swim in the pool every day.
7. The books are heavy.
8. I called Aunt Martha last week.
9. China produces a lot of green tea.
10. Mr. Smith's dog barks at night.

Answers on page 235.

LESSON 57

NEW WORD   καί

MEANING   *and*

PRONUNCIATION TIP: This word contains the αι diphthong which sounds like the English word *eye*. Therefore the word καί will rhyme with *sky, pie,* and *try.*

Here's an example of how καί can be used in a sentence:

εἰμὶ διδάσκαλος καὶ ἰᾱτρός. *(I am a teacher and a doctor.)*

EXERCISES

1. φιλόσοφος καὶ ἰᾱτρός εἰμι.

2. εἰμὶ ὁ διδάσκαλος καὶ ὁ ἰᾱτρός.

3. ὁ Κάδμος εἰμί.

4. Τηλέμαχός εἰμι.

5. εἰμὶ ὁ γεωργός.

6. εἰμὶ γεωργὸς καὶ φιλόσοφος.

7. φιλόσοφός εἰμι καὶ ἰᾱτρός.

8. εἰμὶ Κάδμος.

9. ἰᾱτρός εἰμι.

10. Ἀλέξανδρός εἰμι.

Answers on page 235.

LESSON 58

NEW WORD   οὐκ

MEANING   *not*

PRONUNCIATION TIP: This one-syllable word rhymes with *spook* and *fluke*. Notice that it starts with the diphthong ου and a smooth breathing.

In Greek, if you want to say that something is not happening, you can use the word οὐκ which means *not*. Generally speaking, οὐκ will come right before the verb, like this:

οὐκ εἰμὶ Ἀλέξανδρος. *(I am not Alexander.)*

The word οὐκ doesn't have its own accent. But when it comes immediately before some (not all) enclitics it can take an accent. Then it will look like this, with a smooth breathing and an accent parked next to each other above the *upsilon*.

οὔκ

EXERCISES

1. οὐκ εἰμί.

2. Ἀλέξανδρος οὐκ εἰμί.

3. οὐκ εἰμὶ φιλόσοφος.

4. οὐκ εἰμὶ ἰᾱτρός.

5. εἰμὶ ἰᾱτρὸς καὶ διδάσκαλος.

6. οὐκ εἰμὶ ὁ Κάδμος.

7. γεωργός εἰμι.

8. οὐκ εἰμὶ διδάσκαλος.

9. ὁ Τηλέμαχός εἰμι.

10. εἰμὶ Κάδμος.

Answers on page 235.

LESSON 59

NEW WORD   εἶ

MEANING   *you are*

PRONUNCIATION TIP: This word consists of the ει diphthong and a smooth breathing. You can pronounce it like the vowel sound in the word *eight*. Unlike εἰμί, the verb εἶ is not an enclitic, so it will keep its accent.

In English, it takes two words to say *you are*. In Greek, it takes only one: εἶ. The pronoun *you* is embedded in the verb itself. This verb is singular in the sense that you would use it when talking to only one person.

Here's an example of how εἶ could be used in a sentence:

εἶ γεωργός.   *(You are a farmer.)*

EXERCISES

1. οὐκ εἶ Κάδμος.

2. εἶ ἰᾱτρός.

3. ἰᾱτρὸς εἶ.

4. εἶ γεωργὸς καὶ διδάσκαλος.

5. οὐκ εἰμὶ φιλόσοφος.

6. εἰμὶ Ἀλέξανδρος.

7. οὐκ εἰμὶ ὁ Τηλέμαχος.

8. εἶ φιλόσοφος.

9. οὐκ εἰμὶ Κάδμος.

10. φιλόσοφος καὶ ἰᾱτρός εἰμι.

Answers on page 235.

73

LESSON 60

MOVABLE NU

The human mouth likes to say words in a smooth, coordinated fashion. For this reason, we sometimes make small adjustments to the spelling and pronunciation of words to make them easier to pronounce. An example of this would be the English words *a* and *an*. They are actually two variations of the same word—the difference is that *a* comes before words that begin with a consonant sound and *an* comes before words that begin with a vowel sound. Why? This is because it is easier for your mouth to pronounce sounds clearly and distinctly when the sounds alternate between consonant sounds and vowel sounds.

Try to experience this for yourself by saying the following word combination:

A acorn

When you say *a acorn*, you must pronounce two vowel sounds in a row, which can be awkward to pronounce clearly. The solution to this problem is to introduce the word *acorn* with the article *an*, like this:

An acorn

This creates a vowel-consonant-vowel pattern which is much easier to pronounce. Try this word combination, too:

An nut

When you say *an nut*, you have two *n* sounds in a row, which is difficult to pronounce clearly. The solution to this problem is to introduce the word *nut* with the article *a*.

A nut

Again, it is easier now because there is a vowel-consonant-vowel pattern.

The reason I'm telling you all this is that soon we will see this same kind of thing in ancient Greek. In fact, in the next lesson we will learn a new verb that means *he is, she is,* or *it is.* This verb can be spelled with the letter *nu* at the end, like this…

$$\dot{\epsilon}\sigma\tau\acute{\iota}\nu$$

…or without the letter *nu* at the end, like this:

$$\dot{\epsilon}\sigma\tau\acute{\iota}$$

Either way, it's the same word—the only difference is that sometimes the letter *nu* is there at the end, and sometimes it's not there.

This letter *nu*, that can appear or disappear, is called *movable nu*. If a word has a movable *nu* at the end, the spelling depends on what comes next (just as with the English words *a* and *an*). If the next word starts with a consonant, you spell this word $\dot{\epsilon}\sigma\tau\acute{\iota}$ and if the next word starts with a vowel you spell this word $\dot{\epsilon}\sigma\tau\acute{\iota}\nu$. Also, you spell it $\dot{\epsilon}\sigma\tau\acute{\iota}\nu$ if it is the last word in a sentence. If a word with a movable *nu* is being displayed somewhere and is not part of a sentence, the letter *nu* will be shown in parentheses, like this: $\dot{\epsilon}\sigma\tau\acute{\iota}(\nu)$.

LESSON 61

NEW WORD　　ἐστί(ν)

MEANING　　*he is, she is, it is*

PRONUNCIATION TIP: This word has a movable *nu*, so if the next word begins with a consonant, this word will be spelled ἐστί. But if the next word starts with a vowel, or if it is the last word in a sentence, it will be spelled ἐστίν. This word is an enclitic, so it may lose its accent depending on what comes before it. Also, under certain circumstances, the accent may move to the first syllable.

In English, it takes two words to say *he is, she is,* or *it is.* But in Greek, it only takes one. Like all Greek verbs, there is a pronoun embedded in the verb. So the word ἐστί(ν) can be translated as *he is, she is,* or *it is.* Here's an example of this kind of use of ἐστί(ν).

γεωργός ἐστιν.

Again, ἐστί(ν) can be translated as *he is, she is,* or *it is.* This means that the example sentence shown above could be translated as *He is a farmer, She is a farmer,* or *It is a farmer.* We really don't know who this sentence is talking about because we don't know its context. The important thing I want you to notice here is that there is a pronoun included in the word ἐστί(ν) that you can use in your translation—and that pronoun is the subject of the sentence. Therefore if you translate the sentence as *He is a farmer,* then the word *he* is the subject.

But other times, you won't need to use the pronoun that is included in ἐστί(ν) because there is a separate noun that is the subject of the sentence. For example, the word *Alexander* is the subject of this sentence:

Ἀλέξανδρός ἐστι γεωργός.

In that sentence, the subject is Alexander, so there is no need to use the pronoun *he* that is included in ἐστί(ν). If you included the pronoun *he* in your

76

translation, it would say *Alexander he is a farmer* which wouldn't make any sense because the word *he* would be unnecessary. So when there is a separate word to be the subject of the sentence, you should leave out the pronoun and translate ἐστί(ν) simply as *is*. Therefore this sentence would be translated as *Alexander is a farmer.*

And here is yet another reminder that a Greek sentence will not always follow the same word order that you would expect in an English sentence. For example, if you want to say that Alexander is a philosopher, you could put the word φιλόσοφος right next to the word Ἀλέξανδρος, like this:

Ἀλέξανδρος φιλόσοφός ἐστιν. *(Alexander is a philosopher.)*

As you progress in your Greek studies, you will learn more about Greek word order and how it can communicate meaning. Also, you'll learn much more about Greek pronouns. But for now, I'll just give you simple sentences to practice with.

EXERCISES

1. ὁ Ἀλέξανδρός ἐστι διδάσκαλος.

2. Τηλέμαχος ἰᾱτρός ἐστιν.

3. Κάδμος οὐκ ἔστι γεωργός.

4. ὁ γεωργὸς οὐκ ἔστιν ἰᾱτρός.

5. ἰᾱτρὸς εἶ.

6. οὐκ εἰμὶ Τηλέμαχος.

7. οὐκ εἶ Κάδμος.

8. εἰμὶ γεωργὸς καὶ διδάσκαλος.

9. ὁ φιλόσοφός ἐστι διδάσκαλος.

10. οὐκ εἶ ἰᾱτρός.

Answers on page 235.

77

LESSON 62

NEW WORD   στρατηγός

MEANING   *general*

PRONUNCIATION TIP: This word has three syllables with the accent on the last syllable. It sounds like *stra-teh-GOHSS*.

The word στρατηγός, like many Greek words, is made up of two smaller words. The στρατ- part of the word comes from the Greek word στρατός which means *army*. The -ηγός part of the word comes from the Greek verb ἄγω which means *I lead*. Therefore the word στρατηγός literally means *army-leader*. But it is usually translated into English as *general*. In English we have several related words such as *strategy*, *strategic*, and *strategem*.

Remember that word order in Greek can be flexible, so don't expect the words in a Greek sentence to be in the same order as they would be in a corresponding English sentence.

EXERCISES

1. ὁ στρατηγός εἰμι.

2. εἰμὶ στρατηγός.

3. εἰμὶ ὁ στρατηγός.

4. στρατηγός εἰμι.

5. ὁ Ἀλέξανδρός ἐστιν ὁ στρατηγός.

6. οὐκ εἶ στρατηγός.

7. ὁ ἰᾱτρὸς οὐκ ἔστιν γεωργός.

78

8. Κάδμος οὐκ ἔστι στρατηγός.

9. Τηλέμαχός ἐστι ἰᾱτρὸς καὶ διδάσκαλος.

10. ὁ φιλόσοφος οὐκ ἔστιν ἰᾱτρός.

Answers on page 235.

LESSON 63

SINGULAR AND PLURAL

Singular means one of something. *Plural* means more than one of something. In grammar, this characteristic of being singular or plural is called *number*.

In the exercises below, try to figure out what the subject of the sentence is. Then, decide if the subject is singular or plural.

EXERCISES

1. The car is red.
2. We have ice cream cones.
3. Flowers are pretty.
4. I like blueberry pie.
5. They like hamburgers.
6. Jimmy will go to school tomorrow.
7. The team has five players.
8. Mary is a good clarinet player.
9. In France, they speak French.
10. Many houses are on our street.

Answers on page 235.

LESSON 64

NEW WORD   γεωργοί

MEANING   *farmers*

PRONUNCIATION TIP: This word ends with the οι diphthong which rhymes with *toy*, *boy*, and *soy*. Therefore this word sounds like *geh-ohr-GOY*.

In English, we make a noun plural by changing its ending, mostly by adding the letter *s*. In ancient Greek, we also change the ending of a noun to make it plural. All the nouns you know so far can be made plural by changing the ending to οι, like this:

γεωργός ⟶ γεωργοί

Therefore the word γεωργοί means *farmers*.

As you translate these exercises, look carefully at the endings. Can you determine which ones are singular and which ones are plural?

EXERCISES

1. γεωργός

2. γεωργοί

3. διδάσκαλος

4. διδάσκαλοι

5. ἰᾱτρός

6. ἰᾱτροί

7. φιλόσοφος

8. φιλόσοφοι

9. στρατηγός

10. στρατηγοί

Answers on page 236.

LESSON 65

NEW WORD   οἱ

MEANING   *the* (plural)

PRONUNCIATION TIP: This short word consists of the οι diphthong and a rough breathing, so it sounds like *hoy*.

In English, the definite article (the word *the*) is always the same. Even if the noun it introduces is plural, the word *the* stays the same.

- the cat
- the cats

Whether the word *cat* was singular or plural, the article *the* stayed the same.

But in ancient Greek, the article changes along with the noun it introduces. If a noun is singular, its article also must be singular. If a noun is plural, its article also must be plural. Our new word for this lesson is οἱ which is just like ὁ except plural.

Here is a singular noun with a singular definite article:

ὁ γεωργός *(the farmer)*

Now let's make it plural, using our new plural definite article to introduce the plural noun.

οἱ γεωργοί *(the farmers)*

You'll see this concept over and over as you go along—that in ancient Greek, a definite article always must have the same characteristics as the noun it introduces. This concept is called *agreement,* and we will talk about it more in upcoming lessons.

In the exercises below, watch out for plural nouns with the $-οι$ ending. Not all of the exercises are complete sentences!

EXERCISES

1. ὁ γεωργός

2. οἱ γεωργοί

3. ὁ ἰᾱτρός

4. οἱ ἰᾱτροί

5. ὁ διδάσκαλος καὶ οἱ γεωργοί

6. ὁ στρατηγός ἐστι φιλόσοφος.

7. διδάσκαλος εἶ καὶ φιλόσοφος.

8. οὐκ εἰμὶ γεωργός.

9. Κάδμος στρατηγός ἐστιν.

10. Τηλέμαχος οὐκ ἔστι στρατηγός.

Answers on page 236.

LESSON 66

NEW WORD   *ἐσμέν*

MEANING   *we are*

PRONUNCIATION TIP: This word sounds like *ess-MEN*. But since it is an enclitic, it may lose its accent depending on what comes before it.

Our new word for this lesson is a plural verb, so it refers to more than one person.

Now that you know a plural verb, we can put together a complete sentence with a plural noun, like this one:

ἐσμὲν γεωργοί.   *(We are farmers.)*

EXERCISES

1. ἐσμέν.

2. οὐκ ἐσμὲν οἱ γεωργοί.

3. γεωργοί ἐσμεν.

4. οἱ ἰᾱτροὶ οὐκ ἐσμέν.

5. ἐσμὲν διδάσκαλοι καὶ ἰᾱτροί.

6. Κάδμος οὐκ ἔστι στρατηγός.

7. Τηλέμαχος οὐκ εἶ.

8. στρατηγὸς καὶ φιλόσοφός εἰμι.

9. ὁ Ἀλέξανδρός ἐστιν ὁ στρατηγός.

10. ὁ στρατηγός ἐστι γεωργός.

Answers on page 236.

LESSON 67

NEW WORD   ἐστέ

MEANING   *you are* (plural)

PRONUNCIATION TIP: This word sounds like *es-TEH*. But since it is an enclitic, it may lose its accent depending on what comes before it.

You already know that the word εἶ means *you are*. We use εἶ when speaking to one person. ἐστέ also means *you are*, but with one important difference: ἐστέ is plural. The English word *you* can refer to one person or more than one person. But other languages such as ancient Greek, Latin, and French have different words for singular *you* and plural *you*.

As English speakers, sometimes we use expressions such as *you guys, you people,* or *yinz* (if you live near Pittsburgh) to try to make it clear that we are talking to more than one person. In the southeastern United States, where this author is from, we often use the contraction *y'all* to address more than one person (never just one). *Y'all* is simply a contraction of the words *you* and *all*. *Y'all* rhymes with *hall, ball,* and *fall*.

In this book I will use the word *y'all* to represent the plural *you* in English. So, in the answer key, ἐστέ will be translated as *y'all are*. If you are from the southeastern United States, using this word will be easy for you. If not, y'all will get used to it after using it a few times.

EXERCISES

1. ἐστέ.

2. ἐστὲ διδάσκαλοι.

3. ἐστὲ ἰᾱτροί.

4. οἱ φιλόσοφοί ἐστε.

5. διδάσκαλοι οὐκ ἐσμέν.

6. οὐκ ἐσμὲν οἱ ἰᾱτροί.

7. ὁ στρατηγὸς εἶ.

8. Τηλέμαχος διδάσκαλός ἐστιν καὶ φιλόσοφος.

9. οὐκ εἰμὶ γεωργός.

10. ὁ Κάδμος οὐκ ἔστι γεωργός.

Answers on page 236.

LESSON 68

NEW WORD   εἰσί(ν)

MEANING   *they are*

PRONUNCIATION TIP: This word has a movable *nu,* so if the next word begins with a consonant, it will be spelled εἰσί. But if this is the last word in a sentence or if the next word starts with a vowel, this word will be spelled εἰσίν. This word is an enclitic, so it may lose its accent depending on what comes before it.

In English, it takes two words to say *they are.* But in Greek, it only takes one: the word εἰσί(ν). Like all Greek verbs, there is a pronoun embedded in the verb. So the word εἰσί(ν) can be translated as *they are.* Here's an example of this kind of use of εἰσί(ν).

> γεωργοί εἰσιν

Again, εἰσί can be translated as *they are.* This means that the example sentence shown above could be translated as *They are farmers.* We really don't know who this sentence is talking about because we don't know its context. The important thing I want you to notice here is that there is a pronoun included in the word εἰσί(ν) that you can use in your translation—and that pronoun is the subject of the sentence. Therefore if you translate the sentence as *They are farmers,* then the word *they* is the subject.

But other times, you won't need to use the pronoun that is included in εἰσί(ν) because there is a separate noun that is the subject of the sentence. For example, the word *teachers* is the subject of this sentence:

> οἱ διδάσκαλοί εἰσι γεωργοί.

In that sentence, the teachers are the subject of the sentence, so there is no need to use the pronoun *they* that is included in εἰσί(ν). If you included the pronoun

86

they in your translation, it would say *The teachers they are farmers* which wouldn't make any sense because the word *they* would be unnecessary. So when there is a separate word to be the subject of the sentence, you should leave out the pronoun and translate εἰσί(ν) simply as *are*. Therefore this sentence would be translated as *The teachers are farmers*.

And, as always, remember that in a Greek sentence, the words won't always be in the same order as you would expect them to be in an English sentence.

EXERCISES

1. οἱ διδάσκαλοί εἰσιν ἰᾱτροί.

2. Τηλέμαχος καὶ Ἀλέξανδρος οὐκ εἰσὶν ἰᾱτροί.

3. οἱ φιλόσοφοί εἰσι διδάσκαλοι.

4. ἐσμὲν στρατηγοί.

5. γεωργοὶ οὐκ ἐστέ.

6. ὁ ἰᾱτρός ἐστι γεωργός.

7. Κάδμος διδάσκαλός ἐστιν.

8. οὐκ εἶ στρατηγός.

9. Ἀλέξανδρος οὐκ ἔστι διδάσκαλος.

10. γεωργοί ἐσμεν.

Answers on page 236.

LESSON 69

PERSON

Pronouns and verbs can be in the first person, second person, or third person. This characteristic tells us about the viewpoint or aspect from which the action is being viewed.

- ❏ Pronouns and verbs that refer to *I* or *we* are first person (the person who is speaking).

- ❏ Pronouns and verbs that refer to *you*, either singular or plural, are second person (the person or people to whom the speaker is speaking). In this book we will use *y'all* for the second person plural to help distinguish it from the second person singular.

- ❏ Pronouns and verbs that refer to *he, she, it,* or *they* are third person (the person, thing, people, or things being spoken about).

The following chart should help illustrate this concept:

	Singular	Plural
First Person	I	we
Second Person	you	you
Third Person	he, she, it	they

y'all

If we put all the ancient Greek verbs you know in a chart like the one above, it would look like this:

	SINGULAR	PLURAL
FIRST PERSON	εἰμί	ἐσμέν
SECOND PERSON	εἶ	ἐστέ
THIRD PERSON	ἐστί(ν)	εἰσί(ν)

At this point you need to memorize these verbs and practice saying them until you can say them confidently.

In the exercises below, we have a triple challenge for you. First, determine what the subject of each sentence is. Then, determine if the subject is first person, second person, or third person. Finally, determine whether the subject is singular or plural.

EXERCISES

1. I am hungry.
2. You are a nice person.
3. She is very smart.
4. We are going to the park.
5. Y'all have a beautiful home.
6. They eat lunch at Aunt Martha's house every Sunday.
7. He is a tennis player.
8. It is a history book.
9. Y'all really know how to throw a party.
10. The flowers in your garden are pretty.

Answers on page 236.

LESSON 70

AGREEMENT

In ancient Greek, words work together to create meaningful sentences. In Greek grammar there is an important concept that you need to know about called *agreement*. Agreement means that there are certain situations in which two words must have the same characteristics in order for them to be able to work together. Let's learn more about agreement by studying some of the specific situations in which words must agree with each other.

NOUN AND ARTICLE

A noun and its article must both be singular or both be plural. In the example below, notice that both the article and noun are plural.

οἱ στρατηγοί

The words οἱ and στρατηγοί are both plural, so they agree in number (the word *number* here is the grammatical term that refers to whether something is singular or plural). But what's wrong with this example?

ὁ στρατηγοί

That example doesn't make any sense because ὁ is a singular article and στρατηγοί is plural. Call the grammar police!

SUBJECT AND VERB

A subject and verb must agree in number. In this example, observe that both the subject and verb are singular.

εἰμὶ γεωργός.

In that example, γεωργός and εἰμί are both singular, so they agree and the sentence makes sense. It means *I am a farmer*. But do you see anything wrong with this sentence?

εἰμὶ γεωργοί.

This sentence doesn't make any sense because εἰμί is singular and γεωργοί is plural. It translates to *I am farmers*! What a mess!

This lesson has been a very rudimentary introduction to the idea of agreement in Greek grammar. This basic information will do for now—but as you continue studying Greek, you will learn several other ways in which various kinds of words must agree with each other. You'll never outgrow the need to pay attention to agreement—it is every bit as important to advanced Greek students as it is to beginners.

LESSON 71

MORE ABOUT PRONOUNS

At this point in the book you have some good experience working with Greek verbs. You know that Greek verbs really have two ingredients—a pronoun and a verb. This means that there is a pronoun embedded in each of the verbs that you know. For example, the verb εἰμί includes the pronoun *I* and the verb *am*, all in one word.

But wait...there's more! In addition to these pronouns that are embedded in verbs, ancient Greek also has separate words for pronouns. This means that in Greek there is a separate pronoun that means *I*, another pronoun that means *you*, another one that means *we*, and another one that means *y'all*—and many other pronouns, too.

Now you may be wondering: *If Greek verbs already include pronouns, why does the Greek language need to have separate pronoun words, too?* To answer this question, let's take a moment to think about pronouns in general, and how they are useful to writers and speakers.

WHAT DO PRONOUNS DO, EXACTLY?

The basic function of a pronoun is that it takes the place of a noun—in fact, that's the literal meaning of the word *pronoun.* In both written and spoken language, pronouns can be useful in several ways. Let's examine some of the ways pronouns can help people express themselves.

One way that pronouns can be useful is that they allow us to avoid repeating the names of people or things. Take this sentence for example:

Michael is wearing a new shirt. Michael bought it yesterday.

A bit repetitive, wouldn't you say? Now, let's try it this way:

Michael is wearing a new shirt. He bought it yesterday.

In that example, instead of repeating the word *Michael* in the second sentence, we used the pronoun *he* to take the place of the word *Michael.* In this way, we avoided repeating his name unnecessarily.

A pronoun can also help you to clarify the meaning of a sentence. Compare these two sentences and see if you notice anything in particular.

- While walking to work, thinking about Greek, I stopped for coffee.
- I, while walking to work, thinking about Greek, stopped for coffee.

Which of those two sentences was easier to understand? Probably the second one, because the pronoun *I* is at the beginning of the sentence. Since the pronoun *I* is at the beginning, it is clear right from the start who is doing the action in the sentence. But in the first sentence, because the pronoun is delayed until the end, it isn't clear at first who is doing the action—you have to wait a little to find out who is doing the walking and thinking (and coffee drinking). Therefore, I would argue that in the second sentence, putting the pronoun first makes the meaning of the sentence clearer to the reader or listener.

Here's another way pronouns can clarify the meaning of a sentence. Compare these two sentences and see if you notice anything.

- Broccoli tastes terrible.
- To me, broccoli tastes terrible.

In the first sentence, someone is making a universal statement about broccoli—the statement is not limited in any way. Presumably, the speaker thinks that broccoli tastes terrible to everyone. But in the second sentence, the speaker uses the pronoun *me* to limit the statement. The speaker is saying that while others might enjoy the taste of broccoli, to this particular speaker, it tastes terrible. So again, a pronoun helps to clarify the sentence, enabling speakers and writers to express themselves more precisely and clearly.

Here's one last example—compare these sentences and see if anything comes to mind.

- Mistakes were made.
- I made mistakes.

In the first sentence, the speaker has arranged the words in such a way that there is no pronoun needed. The verb is a passive verb, so the sentence has a certain impersonal kind of sound to it. If you say "Mistakes were made," you can acknowledge that someone made a mistake without revealing exactly who it was that made the mistake (I've seen politicians say this kind of thing on TV and in the newspaper). But in the second sentence, the speaker uses the pronoun *I* to show specifically who made the mistakes, taking personal responsibility for them. So again, a pronoun adds clarity, emphasis, and expressiveness to the sentence.

The point here is that pronouns can be useful in any language, including ancient Greek. Over the next few lessons you will learn a few Greek pronouns that you can use with the verbs you know.

LESSON 72

NEW WORD   ἐγώ

MEANING   *I*

PRONUNCIATION TIP: This word sounds like *eh-GOH*, with the stress on the second syllable.

By itself, εἰμί means *I am*. It doesn't need any help from a pronoun to say *I am* because the pronoun *I* is embedded in the verb itself. However, you can use the pronoun ἐγώ along with εἰμί to clarify or emphasize the meaning of εἰμί.

Here are a few examples of how the pronoun ἐγώ can be used with εἰμί in a sentence. All three examples mean the same thing: *I am a teacher.* Notice the flexible word order.

- ἐγώ εἰμι διδάσκαλος.
- ἐγὼ διδάσκαλός εἰμι.
- διδάσκαλος ἐγώ εἰμι.

EXERCISES

1. ἐγώ

2. εἰμί.

3. ἐγώ εἰμι.

4. ἐγώ εἰμι Ἀλέξανδρος.

5. ἐγὼ Κάδμος εἰμί.

6. φιλόσοφος ἐγώ εἰμι.

7. οἱ ἰᾱτροί ἐστε.

8. Τηλέμαχος καὶ Ἀλέξανδρος οὐκ εἰσὶ διδάσκαλοι.

9. οὐκ ἐσμὲν φιλόσοφοι.

10. ὁ Κάδμος οὐκ ἔστιν ὁ στρατηγός.

Answers on page 236.

94

LESSON 73

NEW WORD σύ

MEANING *you*

PRONUNCIATION TIP: Remember that the letter *upsilon* is pronounced like the *ee* in *feet*, but with rounded lips.

The verb εἶ doesn't need any help from a pronoun to say *you are* because the pronoun *you* is embedded in the verb. But you can use the pronoun σύ along with εἶ to clarify or emphasize the meaning of εἶ, as in this example:

σὺ γεωργὸς εἶ. *(You are a farmer.)*

EXERCISES

1. σύ

2. σὺ εἶ Τηλέμαχος.

3. σὺ οὐκ εἶ γεωργός.

4. ἐγώ εἰμι στρατηγός.

5. ὁ Κάδμος ἐστὶν ἰᾱτρός.

6. Ἀλέξανδρος οὐκ ἔστιν ἰᾱτρός.

7. ὁ γεωργὸς οὐκ ἔστι στρατηγός.

8. οὐκ ἐστὲ διδάσκαλοι.

9. ἐσμὲν διδάσκαλοι καὶ φιλόσοφοι.

10. Ἀλέξανδρος καὶ Τηλέμαχος διδάσκαλοί εἰσιν.

Answers on page 236.

LESSON 74

NEW WORD   ἡμεῖς

MEANING   *we*

PRONUNCIATION TIP: This two-syllable word starts with a rough breathing. The stress is on the second syllable, which contains the ϵι diphthong. Therefore this word sounds something like *heh-MACE*.

By itself, ἐσμέν means *we are*. It doesn't need any help from a pronoun to say *we are* because the pronoun *we* is embedded in the verb itself. However, you can use the pronoun ἡμεῖς along with ἐσμέν to clarify or strengthen the meaning of ἐσμέν.

EXERCISES

1. ἡμεῖς

2. ἐσμέν.

3. ἡμεῖς ἐσμεν.

4. ἐσμὲν ἡμεῖς.

5. ἡμεῖς ἐσμεν γεωργοί.

6. ἐστὲ διδάσκαλοι.

7. οἱ γεωργοὶ οὐκ εἰσὶ στρατηγοί.

8. σὺ ἰᾱτρὸς καὶ διδάσκαλος εἶ.

9. ἐγὼ φιλόσοφός εἰμι.

10. ὁ στρατηγός ἐστι φιλόσοφος.

Answers on page 237.

LESSON 75

NEW WORD   ὑμεῖς

MEANING   *y'all*

PRONUNCIATION TIP: Remember that the letter *upsilon* is pronounced like the *ee* in *feet*, but with rounded lips. The stress is on the second syllable, which contains the εἰ diphthong, so this word sounds like *hoo-MACE*.

By itself, ἐστέ means *y'all are*. It doesn't need any help from a pronoun to say *y'all are* because the pronoun *y'all* is embedded in the verb itself. However, you can use the pronoun ὑμεῖς along with ἐστέ to clarify or strengthen the meaning of ἐστέ.

The pronouns ὑμεῖς *(y'all)* and ἡμεῖς *(we)* are very similar. In fact, they differ by only one letter! ὑμεῖς starts with an *upsilon* while ἡμεῖς starts with an *eta*. So don't mix them up!

EXERCISES

1. ὑμεῖς

2. ὑμεῖς γεωργοί ἐστε.

3. ἡμεῖς ἰᾱτροί ἐσμεν.

4. ὑμεῖς οὐκ ἐστὲ φιλόσοφοι.

5. οἱ στρατηγοὶ οὐκ εἰσὶν ἰᾱτροί.

6. Κάδμος ἐστὶ διδάσκαλος.

7. Τηλέμαχός ἐστι γεωργὸς καὶ στρατηγός.

8. ὁ ἰᾱτρὸς γεωργὸς οὐκ ἔστιν.

9. ἐγὼ Ἀλέξανδρος οὐκ εἰμί.

10. σὺ στρατηγὸς εἶ.

Answers on page 237.

LESSON 76

NEW WORD   ἔμπορος

MEANING   *merchant*

PRONUNCIATION TIP: This word begins with the letter *epsilon* and a smooth breathing. The accent is on the first syllable, so this word sounds something like *EMM-poh-rohs*.

Our new word for this lesson means *merchant,* as in someone who buys and sells things. It's related to our English word *emporium* which is any kind of large store.

EXERCISES

1. οὐκ εἰμὶ ἔμπορος.

2. ἡμεῖς ἐσμεν ἔμποροι.

3. Τηλέμαχος καὶ Ἀλέξανδρος ἔμποροί εἰσιν.

4. στρατηγὸς εἶ.

5. ὁ Κάδμος οὐκ ἔστιν ὁ ἰᾱτρός.

6. ἐγώ εἰμι ὁ Ἀλέξανδρος.

7. ὑμεῖς γεωργοί ἐστε.

8. οἱ στρατηγοὶ οὐκ εἰσὶ φιλόσοφοι.

9. σὺ οὐκ εἶ ἔμπορος.

10. Ἀλέξανδρος στρατηγός ἐστιν.

Answers on page 237.

LESSON 77

ACTION VERBS

In this book we have only been working with verbs of being or existing—verbs such as *am, is,* and *are.* So far, you have seen lots of sentences like this one:

> Alexander is a farmer.

In that sentence, the verb is the word *is.* That's a verb of being, so in that sentence, Alexander isn't really doing any action—instead, he's just being a farmer.

But at this point in the book, we are going to start working with action verbs in Greek. Action verbs are verbs that show that someone is doing some kind of activity. Examples of action verbs are verbs such as *walk, talk, run, write,* and *swim.* Soon, when you learn some Greek action verbs, we will be able to make sentences like these:

- They <u>run</u>.
- Patricia <u>is reading</u>.
- You <u>write</u>.

So get ready for action! Over the next few lessons, you'll learn your very first Greek action verb.

LESSON 78

ACTION VERBS & THE PRESENT TENSE

Did you know that there is more than one flavor of present tense verb? Let's take a moment to examine the different ways to express present tense action in English.

In English, you might see a sentence like this:

I speak Greek.

Even though you may not be speaking Greek at this very moment, it is still a current event—therefore, we use the present tense to express it. This kind of present tense is called the *simple present*. Contrast that with this similar English sentence:

I am speaking Greek.

In this sentence, the verb is really two words—the words *am* and *speaking*. When you express the present tense in this way, it has a different shade of meaning. Here, you are saying that at this very moment you are speaking the Greek language— the action is happening right now! This kind of present tense is called the *present progressive*. It's progressive because the action is in progress.

So how does this relate to Greek verbs? Here's the idea: The Greek verbs that you will see in this book do not correspond exactly to the simple present or the progressive present. They can be translated either way depending on the context. So, when you see a present tense verb in Greek, you'll have to figure out the best way to translate it into English—that is, you'll have to pick either the simple present or the present progressive for your English translation. If you aren't sure which one to use, try them both. One will probably sound more natural than the other in that particular context.

LESSON 79

NEW WORD   τρέχω

MEANING   *I run, I am running*

PRONUNCIATION TIP: Remember that the letter *chi* represents a light, gentle scraping sound in the back of the mouth.

This is an exciting lesson because you are now learning your very first action verb in Greek: τρέχω. As I mentioned in the last lesson, present tense Greek verbs like this one can be translated into English in more than one way. The verb τρέχω can be translated using the simple present *(I run)* or the present progressive *(I am running)*. In the answer key, I will generally translate action verbs with the present progressive unless for some reason the simple present sounds more natural.

Like verbs of being, action verbs have pronouns embedded in them. For example, the verb τρέχω by itself means *I run*, without the help of any additional pronoun. That's because the pronoun *I* is included in the verb itself. However, you can use the pronoun ἐγώ along with τρέχω to clarify and strengthen its meaning.

EXERCISES

1. τρέχω.

2. ἐγὼ τρέχω.

3. τρέχω ἐγώ.

4. σὺ ἔμπορος εἶ.

5. ἡμεῖς ἐσμεν ἔμποροι.

6. ὁ στρατηγός ἐστι γεωργός.

7. οἱ φιλόσοφοί εἰσιν ἰᾱτροί.

8. ἔμποροι καὶ γεωργοί ἐσμεν.

9. Ἀλέξανδρος καὶ Κάδμος οὐκ εἰσὶ στρατηγοί.

10. ὑμεῖς διδάσκαλοί ἐστε.

Answers on page 237.

LESSON 80

MORE ABOUT οὐκ

Sometimes Greek words have variations in spelling. You already have some experience working with spelling variations—for example, the movable *nu* at the end of the words ἐστί(ν) and εἰσί(ν) can stay or go depending on whether the next word starts with a vowel or a consonant.

The word οὐκ can also have variations in spelling. Depending on what the next word is, the *kappa* at the end of the word οὐκ can go away or change into the letter *chi*. Here is how it works:

When the word οὐκ comes before a vowel with a smooth breathing, the *kappa* at the end stays put, like this:

οὐκ εἰμί

And that is what you have seen so far in this book. But if the next word starts with a consonant, the *kappa* at the end of οὐκ goes away, and οὐκ becomes οὐ, like this:

102

οὐ τρέχω.

And if the next word starts with a vowel with a rough breathing, the *kappa* at the end of οὐκ changes into the letter *chi*, like this:

οὐχ ἡμεῖς

This is because it would be difficult to pronounce the hard *k* sound of a *kappa* followed immediately by a rough breathing. You won't see that spelling in this book, but it's a good idea at least to be aware of it.

So the Greek word for *not* can be spelled three ways: οὐκ, οὐ, or οὐχ. It likes to change its spelling because it's a rather not-ty word!

EXERCISES

1. οὐκ εἰμί.

2. οὐ τρέχω.

3. ἐγὼ οὐ τρέχω.

4. οὐκ ἐστὲ διδάσκαλοι.

5. ὁ Τηλέμαχος οὐκ ἔστι φιλόσοφος.

6. οἱ ἔμποροι οὐκ εἰσὶ φιλόσοφοι.

7. ἡμεῖς οὐκ ἐσμὲν ἰᾱτροί.

8. ὑμεῖς ἐστε ἰᾱτροὶ καὶ διδάσκαλοι.

9. ὁ στρατηγὸς οὐκ ἔστιν ἰᾱτρός.

10. σὺ οὐκ εἶ γεωργός.

Answers on page 237.

LESSON 81

NEW WORD   τρέχεις

MEANING   *you run, you are running*

PRONUNCIATION TIP: Remember that the letter *chi* represents a gentle scraping sound in the back of the mouth.

So far, the only form of τρέχω that you know is the first person singular form which is...well ... τρέχω. But now, it's time to start learning the other present tense forms of this new action verb. We will take it slowly and learn them one form at a time. In this lesson we will learn the second person singular form.

	SINGULAR	PLURAL
FIRST PERSON	τρέχω	
SECOND PERSON	(τρέχεις)	
THIRD PERSON		

Over the next few lessons we will gradually fill in this chart with the various forms of τρέχω. I'll circle the new form for each lesson. If you need to review how this verb chart works you can refer back to lesson 69.

Remember that you can use pronouns along with action verbs just as you can with verbs of being. Here's an example sentence to help you get started:

σὺ τρέχεις. *(You are running.)*

EXERCISES

1. τρέχεις.

2. τρέχεις σύ.

3. οὐ τρέχεις.

4. τρέχω ἐγώ.

5. ἐσμὲν ἰᾱτροὶ καὶ διδάσκαλοι.

6. οὐκ εἶ Κάδμος.

7. ὁ ἔμπορός ἐστι στρατηγός.

8. ὑμεῖς ἐστε γεωργοί.

9. οἱ φιλόσοφοί εἰσιν ἰᾱτροὶ καὶ διδάσκαλοι.

10. ἡμεῖς φιλόσοφοί ἐσμεν.

Answers on page 237.

LESSON 82

NEW WORD   τρέχει

MEANING   *he/she/it runs, he/she/it is running*

PRONUNCIATION TIP: This verb, unlike the verb ἐστί(ν), does not have a movable *nu* at the end. It is always just τρέχει no matter what comes after it.

The chart is getting fuller:

	SINGULAR	PLURAL
FIRST PERSON	τρέχω	
SECOND PERSON	τρέχεις	
THIRD PERSON	(τρέχει)	

In English, it takes two words to say *he runs, she runs,* or *it runs*. But in Greek, it only takes one. Like all Greek verbs, there is a pronoun embedded in this verb. So the word τρέχει can be translated as *he runs, she runs,* or *it runs*. Or, you could use the progressive present and translate it as *he is running, she is running,* or *it is running*.

My point here is that by itself, the word τρέχει makes a complete sentence. We don't really know who this sentence is talking about because we don't know its context. The important thing I want you to notice here is that there is a pronoun included in the word τρέχει that you can use in your translation—and that pronoun is the subject of the sentence. Therefore if you translate the sentence as *He runs* or *He is running,* then the word *he* is the subject.

106

But other times, you won't need to use the pronoun that is included in τρέχει because there is a separate noun that is the subject of the sentence. For example, the word *Alexander* is the subject of this sentence:

Ἀλέξανδρος τρέχει.

In that sentence, the subject is Alexander, so there is no need to use the pronoun *he* that is included in τρέχει. If you included the pronoun *he* in your translation, it would say *Alexander he runs* or *Alexander he is running* which wouldn't make any sense because the word *he* would be unnecessary. So when there is a separate word to be the subject of the sentence, you should leave out the pronoun because you don't need it. Therefore this sentence would be translated as *Alexander runs* or *Alexander is running*.

In the answer key, I will generally use the present progressive unless the simple present sounds better for some reason.

EXERCISES

1. ὁ φιλόσοφος τρέχει.

2. Κάδμος οὐ τρέχει.

3. σὺ τρέχεις.

4. ἐγὼ οὐ τρέχω.

5. ἡμεῖς οὐκ ἐσμὲν διδάσκαλοι.

6. Τηλέμαχος καὶ Κάδμος ἔμποροί εἰσιν.

7. ὑμεῖς ἰᾱτροί ἐστε.

8. ὁ γεωργός ἐστι φιλόσοφος.

9. οἱ διδάσκαλοι οὐκ εἰσὶ στρατηγοί.

10. ἐγὼ γεωργός εἰμι.

Answers on page 237.

LESSON 83

NEW WORD   τρέχομεν

MEANING   *we run, we are running*

Here is your first plural form of τρέχω.

	SINGULAR	PLURAL
FIRST PERSON	τρέχω	⬭τρέχομεν⬭
SECOND PERSON	τρέχεις	
THIRD PERSON	τρέχει	

EXERCISES

1. τρέχομεν.

2. οὐ τρέχομεν.

3. τρέχει Ἀλέξανδρος.

4. ὁ ἔμπορος τρέχει.

5. ἐγὼ τρέχω.

6. ἡμεῖς τρέχομεν.

7. Κάδμος οὐκ ἔστιν ἰᾱτρός.

8. σὺ τρέχεις.

108

9. ἐσμὲν φιλόσοφοι καὶ διδάσκαλοι.

10. ὑμεῖς οὐκ ἐστὲ στρατηγοί.

Answers on page 237.

LESSON 84

NEW WORD   τρέχετε

MEANING   *y'all run, y'all are running*

Our chart is almost full!

	SINGULAR	PLURAL
FIRST PERSON	τρέχω	τρέχομεν
SECOND PERSON	τρέχεις	τρέχετε
THIRD PERSON	τρέχει	

Here's an example sentence with τρέχετε:

ὑμεῖς οὐ τρέχετε. *(Y'all are not running.)*

EXERCISES

1. τρέχετε.

2. ὁ Τηλέμαχος οὐ τρέχει.

3. τρέχομεν.

4. ὁ στρατηγὸς οὐκ ἔστι γεωργός.

5. Ἀλέξανδρός ἐστιν ἰᾱτρὸς καὶ ἔμπορος.

6. Τηλέμαχος καὶ Κάδμος εἰσὶ γεωργοί.

7. σὺ διδάσκαλος εἶ.

8. οὐκ ἐσμέν οἱ στρατηγοί.

9. οἱ ἰᾱτροί εἰσι φιλόσοφοι.

10. τρέχω ἐγώ.

Answers on page 238.

LESSON 85

NEW WORD   τρέχουσι(ν)

MEANING   *they run, they are running*

The chart is now full!

	SINGULAR	PLURAL
FIRST PERSON	τρέχω	τρέχομεν
SECOND PERSON	τρέχεις	τρέχετε
THIRD PERSON	τρέχει	τρέχουσι(ν)

In English, it takes two words to say *they run*. But in Greek, it only takes one: τρέχουσι(ν). Like all Greek verbs, there is a pronoun embedded in this verb. So the word τρέχουσι(ν) can be translated as *they run* or *they are running*.

By itself, the word τρέχουσι(ν) makes a complete sentence. We don't really know who this sentence is talking about because we don't know its context. The important thing I want you to notice here is that there is a pronoun included in the word τρέχουσι(ν) that you can use in your translation—and that pronoun is the subject of the sentence. Therefore if you translate the sentence as *They run* or *They are running*, the word *they* is the subject.

But other times, you won't need to use the pronoun that is included in τρέχουσι(ν) because there is a separate noun that is the subject of the sentence. For example, the word *generals* is the subject of this sentence:

οἱ στρατηγοὶ τρέχουσιν.

111

In that sentence, the subject is the generals, so there is no need to use the pronoun *they* that is included in $\tau\rho\acute{\epsilon}\chi o\upsilon\sigma\iota(\nu)$. If you included the pronoun *they* in your translation, it would say *The generals they run* or *The generals they are running* which wouldn't make any sense because the word *they* would be unnecessary. So when there is a separate word to be the subject of the sentence, you should leave out the pronoun. Therefore this sentence would be translated as *The generals are running* or *The generals run*.

EXERCISES

1. τρέχουσιν.

2. οὐ τρέχουσιν οἱ διδάσκαλοι.

3. τρέχετε.

4. τρέχει Τηλέμαχος.

5. οἱ ἔμποροι οὐκ ἐσμέν.

6. ὁ ἰᾱτρός ἐστι γεωργὸς καὶ φιλόσοφος.

7. Ἀλέξανδρος καὶ Κάδμος στρατηγοί εἰσιν.

8. τρέχομεν ἡμεῖς.

9. ἐγὼ τρέχω.

10. σὺ τρέχεις.

Answers on page 238.

LESSON 86

REVIEW

We now know all six present forms of $\epsilon\grave{\iota}\mu\acute{\iota}$ and $\tau\rho\acute{\epsilon}\chi\omega$. Let's review them now. Here is a chart for $\epsilon\grave{\iota}\mu\acute{\iota}$. Notice that both the third person singular and the third person plural have a movable *nu*.

	SINGULAR	PLURAL
FIRST PERSON	$\epsilon\grave{\iota}\mu\acute{\iota}$	$\grave{\epsilon}\sigma\mu\acute{\epsilon}\nu$
SECOND PERSON	$\epsilon\hat{\iota}$	$\grave{\epsilon}\sigma\tau\acute{\epsilon}$
THIRD PERSON	$\grave{\epsilon}\sigma\tau\acute{\iota}(\nu)$	$\epsilon\grave{\iota}\sigma\acute{\iota}(\nu)$

Say all six forms in sequence: $\epsilon\grave{\iota}\mu\acute{\iota}$, $\epsilon\hat{\iota}$, $\grave{\epsilon}\sigma\tau\acute{\iota}(\nu)$, $\grave{\epsilon}\sigma\mu\acute{\epsilon}\nu$, $\grave{\epsilon}\sigma\tau\acute{\epsilon}$, $\epsilon\grave{\iota}\sigma\acute{\iota}(\nu)$. It is best to memorize them. Try to think of what each word means as you say it.

Here is a chart for $\tau\rho\acute{\epsilon}\chi\omega$. Notice that only the third person plural has a movable *nu* while the third person singular does not.

	SINGULAR	PLURAL
FIRST PERSON	$\tau\rho\acute{\epsilon}\chi\omega$	$\tau\rho\acute{\epsilon}\chi\omega\mu\epsilon\nu$
SECOND PERSON	$\tau\rho\acute{\epsilon}\chi\epsilon\iota\varsigma$	$\tau\rho\acute{\epsilon}\chi\epsilon\tau\epsilon$
THIRD PERSON	$\tau\rho\acute{\epsilon}\chi\epsilon\iota$	$\tau\rho\acute{\epsilon}\chi\omega\sigma\iota(\nu)$

Repeat after me! $\tau\rho\acute{\epsilon}\chi\omega$, $\tau\rho\acute{\epsilon}\chi\epsilon\iota\varsigma$, $\tau\rho\acute{\epsilon}\chi\epsilon\iota$, $\tau\rho\acute{\epsilon}\chi\omega\mu\epsilon\nu$, $\tau\rho\acute{\epsilon}\chi\epsilon\tau\epsilon$, $\tau\rho\acute{\epsilon}\chi\omega\sigma\iota(\nu)$. Again, think of what each word means as you say it. Soon, these verbs will become second nature.

LESSON 87

NEW WORD   οὔποτε

MEANING   *never*

Our new word for this lesson is a combination of two smaller words. As you already know, the word οὐ means *not*. The word ποτέ means something like *at any time* or *ever*. So if you put οὐ and ποτέ together, you get οὔποτε which means *never*—literally, *not at any time* or *not ever*.

Here's an example sentence with οὔποτε.

ἐγὼ οὔποτε τρέχω. *(I never run.)*

EXERCISES

1. ὁ Κάδμος οὔποτε τρέχει.

2. οὔποτε τρέχεις.

3. οὔποτε τρέχομεν.

4. οἱ φιλόσοφοί εἰσι γεωργοί.

5. Ἀλέξανδρος καὶ Τηλέμαχος τρέχουσιν.

6. ὁ διδάσκαλός ἐστι φιλόσοφος.

7. τρέχετε ὑμεῖς.

8. σὺ εἶ γεωργός.

9. οὔποτε τρέχω.

10. ὁ Τηλέμαχός ἐστιν ἔμπορος.

Answers on page 238.

LESSON 88

NEW WORD   ἵππος

MEANING   *horse*

PRONUNCIATION TIP: This word has both a rough breathing and an accent on the first syllable, so it sounds like *HIP-pohs.*

The word *hippopotamus* comes to us from ancient Greek. The *hippo-* part of the word means *horse* (that's our new word for this lesson). The *-potamus* part of the word is from the Greek word ποταμός which means *river*. Therefore the word *hippopotamus* literally means *river-horse.*

Before you try the exercises, let's look at the different ways that you might see the word ἵππος in a sentence:

- ἵππος *(a horse)*
- ἵπποι *(horses)*
- ὁ ἵππος *(the horse)*
- οἱ ἵπποι *(the horses)*

Now saddle up and try these exercises—no horsing around!

EXERCISES

1. ὁ ἵππος τρέχει.

2. οὐκ ἐσμέν ἵπποι.

3. οἱ ἵπποι τρέχουσιν.

4. οὐ τρέχει ὁ ἵππος.

5. ἡμεῖς τρέχομεν.

115

6. Ἀλέξανδρός ἐστι φιλόσοφος καὶ γεωργός.

7. οἱ διδάσκαλοι οὐκ εἰσὶ γεωργοί.

8. σὺ οὔποτε τρέχεις.

9. ἐγὼ τρέχω.

10. τρέχετε ὑμεῖς.

Answers on page 238.

LESSON 89

STEMS AND PERSONAL ENDINGS

Now that you have been working with Greek verbs for a little while, you may have noticed that there is a pattern to the endings of Greek verbs. Let's take a closer look at these endings using the verb τρέχω as an example. For the sake of convenience, here are the six present tense forms of τρέχω again:

	SINGULAR	PLURAL
FIRST PERSON	τρέχω	τρέχομεν
SECOND PERSON	τρέχεις	τρέχετε
THIRD PERSON	τρέχει	τρέχουσι(ν)

Each form of $\tau\rho\acute{\epsilon}\chi\omega$ starts with $\tau\rho\epsilon\chi$-. That part of the verb is called the *stem*. Think of it as a base or a template that stays the same while the rest of the word changes. After the stem, each different form of the verb has its own special, individual ending. If we isolated these endings and put them into a chart, here is what it would look like:

	SINGULAR	PLURAL
FIRST PERSON	$-\omega$	$-o\mu\epsilon\nu$
SECOND PERSON	$-\epsilon\iota\varsigma$	$-\epsilon\tau\epsilon$
THIRD PERSON	$-\epsilon\iota$	$-o\upsilon\sigma\iota(\nu)$

We call these endings *personal endings*. They show whether a verb is first person, second person, or third person, and also whether the verb is singular or plural. Verbs of being don't fully follow this pattern because they are irregular—so what I'm talking about in this lesson pertains mainly to action verbs.

Now that you know about verb stems and personal endings, let's work with them a little and try to build some different forms of $\tau\rho\acute{\epsilon}\chi\omega$. Say, for example, that you wanted to create the second person singular form of $\tau\rho\acute{\epsilon}\chi\omega$. First you would take the stem of the verb, like this:

$\tau\rho\epsilon\chi$-

Then you would figure out what personal ending you need in order to make it second person singular. In this particular case, you need this ending:

$-\epsilon\iota\varsigma$

Now put the stem and the personal ending together, like this:

$\tau\rho\epsilon\chi + \epsilon\iota\varsigma = \tau\rho\acute{\epsilon}\chi\epsilon\iota\varsigma$

117

Just for practice, get a pen and some paper and take some time to experiment with verb stems and personal endings. There are several ways to practice with pen and paper. You could practice writing out the personal endings in an effort to memorize them. Then, you could try to write out the verb stem from memory and add the personal endings from memory. As you write, say the verbs out loud. This kind of practice engages several senses all at once—sight, touch, and hearing. For this reason, it will result in speedy progress for any student of ancient Greek.

Also, this kind of exercise will help you because it will train you to see a Greek verb as something that is made up of different components. That's a skill that will help you both now and in the future when you start working with more complicated Greek verbs.

LESSON 90

NEW WORD αἴλουρος

MEANING *cat*

PRONUNCIATION TIP: This word starts with the αι diphthong, so it sounds like *EYE-loo-rohs*.

Let's "paws" for a moment to learn a new word. The English word *ailurophobia* means *fear of cats*. The *ailuro-* part of the word is from our new word for this lesson. The *-phobia* part of the word is from the Greek word φόβος which means *fear*. Therefore the word *ailurophobia* literally means *cat-fear*.

Before you try the exercises, let's review the different ways you might see the word αἴλουρος in sentences:

- αἴλουρος *(a cat)*
- αἴλουροι *(cats)*
- ὁ αἴλουρος *(the cat)*
- οἱ αἴλουροι *(the cats)*

EXERCISES

1. οὐκ ἐσμὲν αἴλουροι.

2. οἱ αἴλουροι τρέχουσιν.

3. οὔποτε ὁ αἴλουρος τρέχει.

4. οὐκ ἐστὲ αἴλουροι.

5. οὐ τρέχεις.

6. οἱ φιλόσοφοί εἰσιν ἰᾱτροί.

7. ὁ ἵππος οὔποτε τρέχει.

8. ὁ Τηλέμαχός ἐστι διδάσκαλος.

9. τρέχετε.

10. ἡμεῖς τρέχομεν.

Answers on page 238.

LESSON 91

NEW WORD   πολλάκις

MEANING   *often*

Our new word for this lesson, like many Greek words, is a combination of two smaller words. The πολλ- part of the word means *many*. We see this word embedded in English words like *polygon*, *polygamy*, and *polyglot*. The -άκις part of the word is a special suffix that shows how often something happens, like the word *times* in English. So πολλάκις literally means *many times*, conveying the meaning of *often*.

Here's an example sentence with πολλάκις.

Ἀλέξανδρος πολλάκις τρέχει. *(Alexander runs often.)*

EXERCISES

1. οἱ αἴλουροι πολλάκις τρέχουσιν.

2. ὁ ἵππος πολλάκις τρέχει.

3. πολλάκις τρέχω ἐγώ.

4. σὺ οὔποτε τρέχεις.

5. τρέχετε ὑμεῖς.

6. ἡμεῖς οὔποτε τρέχομεν.

7. ὁ αἴλουρος οὔποτε τρέχει.

8. ὁ ἔμπορός ἐστιν ἰατρός.

9. ἡμεῖς στρατηγοί ἐσμεν.

10. Κάδμος ἐστὶ διδάσκαλος.

Answers on page 238.

LESSON 92

NEW WORD   *καθεύδω*

MEANING   *I sleep*

PRONUNCIATION TIP: Notice that this word contains the ευ diphthong. It sounds like the *e* in *leg* followed quickly by the *oo* in *boot*. This word has three syllables, so it sounds something like *ka-THEOO-doe*.

When you learned the verb *τρέχω*, I gave you each form one at a time. But now that you have some experience working with verbs, you don't need that anymore. Therefore from now on when I give you a new verb, I will give you all six present tense forms at once.

Here are the six present forms of *καθεύδω*. The stem is *καθευδ-* so if you add the personal endings to the stem, you'll get the forms in the chart below:

	SINGULAR	PLURAL
FIRST PERSON	*καθεύδω*	*καθεύδομεν*
SECOND PERSON	*καθεύδεις*	*καθεύδετε*
THIRD PERSON	*καθεύδει*	*καθεύδουσι(ν)*

As an exercise, practice writing out the six present tense forms of this verb on a separate sheet of paper. See if you can write the stem and then add the personal endings from memory. It's good practice! You can use the chart shown above to check your work. And whenever you write out Greek words for practice or memorization, don't forget to include accents and breathing marks. These markings are just as important as the letters themselves.

121

Here's an example sentence with our new verb for this lesson:

ὁ αἴλουρος πολλάκις καθεύδει. *(The cat sleeps often.)*

EXERCISES

1. οἱ αἴλουροι πολλάκις καθεύδουσιν.

2. οὔποτε καθεύδουσιν οἱ ἵπποι.

3. οὐ καθεύδομεν.

4. Ἀλέξανδρος πολλάκις καθεύδει.

5. οὔποτε τρέχουσιν οἱ αἴλουροι.

6. Ἀλέξανδρός ἐστιν ἔμπορος.

7. οὔποτε τρέχει ὁ στρατηγός.

8. ὑμεῖς πολλάκις καθεύδετε.

9. σὺ καθεύδεις.

10. ὁ ἔμπορός ἐστι στρατηγός.

Answers on page 238.

LESSON 93

NEW WORD ὅτι

MEANING *because*

PRONUNCIATION TIP: This word starts out with a rough breathing, and the accent is on the first syllable. It sounds something like *HO-tee*.

The Greek word ὅτι can be used in several different ways. It can mean *because*, as seen in the following sentence:

πολλάκις τρέχω <u>ὅτι</u> αἴλουρός εἰμι. *(I often run <u>because</u> I am a cat.)*

If you continue in your Greek studies, you'll learn other ways to use the word ὅτι, but for now just think of it as a word that means *because*.

EXERCISES

1. πολλάκις τρέχω ὅτι ἵππος εἰμί.

2. πολλάκις καθεύδω ὅτι ἐγὼ αἴλουρός εἰμι.

3. οὔποτε τρέχομεν ὅτι στρατηγοί ἐσμεν.

4. Τηλέμαχος οὔποτε τρέχει.

5. ὁ αἴλουρος καθεύδει.

6. οἱ διδάσκαλοι οὔποτε καθεύδουσιν.

7. οὐ τρέχετε.

8. ἰᾱτρός εἰμι.

9. σὺ οὔποτε καθεύδεις.

10. Κάδμος καὶ Ἀλέξανδρος καθεύδουσιν.

Answers on page 238.

LESSON 94

USING CONTEXT TO TRANSLATE THIRD PERSON VERBS

In the last lesson, you learned a new word—the word ὅτι, which means *because*. Now that you know how to say *because* in Greek, we can make sentences that have two parts. For example, if cats could talk, we might have a sentence like this one:

πολλάκις καθεύδω ὅτι αἴλουρός εἰμι. *(I sleep often because I am a cat.)*

This sentence is really two sentences in one. First, there is the part that says *I sleep often*, and then there is the part that says *I am a cat*. The word *because* is a special kind of word called a *conjunction*. A conjunction is a word that can join two sentences together.

Look carefully at this next example sentence. How will you translate the word ἐστί(ν) in the second part of the sentence?

Ἀλέξανδρος πολλάκις καθεύδει ὅτι αἴλουρός ἐστιν.

In the second part of the sentence we have the word ἐστί(ν). As you already know, the word ἐστί(ν) can be translated *he is, she is, it is*, or just *is*. How will you decide how to translate it? There is no word nearby to be the subject of that part of the sentence. Will you use the pronoun included in the verb? Which one?

The answer is that you must look at the context of the sentence. If you look back at the first part of the sentence, you'll see that it is talking about a lazy cat named Alexander and his sleeping habits. Therefore when you get to ἐστί(ν) in the second part of the sentence, you know that it is referring back to Alexander, and that you should translate ἐστί(ν) as *he is*. So for the second part of the sentence, the word *he* is the subject, referring to Alexander.

So when you keep the context of the sentence in mind, it helps you to understand how different parts of the sentence connect together. One part of a sentence or paragraph may give you the context you need to understand another part of the sentence or paragraph. And this is a skill that you will need to develop even more in the future as you translate even more complicated Greek sentences!

124

LESSON 95

NEW WORD   *γράφω*

MEANING   *I write*

We have many English words that are related to our new word for this lesson. It's part of words such as *graphic, biography, photograph, autograph, seismograph, polygraph* and *telegraph*.

The stem is *γραφ-* so if you add the personal endings to the stem, you'll get the forms shown in the chart below:

	SINGULAR	PLURAL
FIRST PERSON	*γράφω*	*γράφομεν*
SECOND PERSON	*γράφεις*	*γράφετε*
THIRD PERSON	*γράφει*	*γράφουσι(ν)*

Here's an example sentence with our new verb for this lesson:

ὁ φιλόσοφος πολλάκις γράφει. (*The philosopher writes often.*)

EXERCISES

1. *πολλάκις γράφω ὅτι φιλόσοφός εἰμι.*

2. *σὺ οὔποτε γράφεις ὅτι αἴλουρος εἶ.*

3. *ἡμεῖς οὔποτε καθεύδομεν ὅτι ἐσμὲν γεωργοί.*

4. ὁ ἔμπορος πολλάκις γράφει.

5. οἱ αἴλουροι πολλάκις καθεύδουσιν.

6. οὔποτε γράφεις ὅτι σὺ ἵππος εἶ.

7. οὔποτε τρέχομεν ὅτι στρατηγοί ἐσμεν.

8. ὁ ἰᾱτρὸς οὐ τρέχει.

9. Ἀλέξανδρος οὐκ ἔστιν ἔμπορος.

10. οἱ διδάσκαλοι καθεύδουσιν.

Answers on page 239.

LESSON 96

NEW WORD   *σπανίως*

MEANING   *seldom*

PRONUNCIATION TIP: This word has three syllables with the stress on the second syllable, so it sounds something like *spah-NEE-ohss*.

Our new word for this lesson means *seldom* or *rarely*. Therefore if I wanted to make a sentence about my exercise habits, I could say this:

     ἐγὼ σπανίως τρέχω. *(I seldom run.)*

EXERCISES

1. ὁ γεωργός σπανίως καθεύδει.

2. ὑμεῖς σπανίως τρέχετε ὅτι στρατηγοί ἐστε.

3. σπανίως γράφομεν ὅτι οὐκ ἐσμὲν φιλόσοφοι.

4. οἱ διδάσκαλοι γράφουσιν.

5. οὔποτε γράφω ὅτι οὐκ εἰμὶ διδάσκαλος.

6. Τηλέμαχος πολλάκις καθεύδει ὅτι αἴλουρός ἐστιν.

7. πολλάκις καθεύδομεν ὅτι ἐσμὲν αἴλουροι.

8. τρέχετε ὑμεῖς.

9. σὺ σπανίως καθεύδεις ὅτι γεωργός εἶ.

10. οἱ αἴλουροι τρέχουσιν.

Answers on page 239.

LESSON 97

NEW WORD   ἀναγιγνώσκω

MEANING   *I read*

PRONUNCIATION TIP: This word has five syllables, and the accent is on the fourth syllable. It sounds something like *ah-nah-gi-GNO-sko*.

The ἀνα- part of this word means *again* while the -γιγνώσκω part means *know* or *recognize*. It's related to English words like *diagnosis* and *agnostic*. Therefore ἀναγιγνώσκω literally means *I know again*, or *I recognize*. And that's why this verb means *to read*—because when you read, you look at words and you recognize them.

The stem is ἀναγιγνωσκ- so if you add the personal endings to the stem, you'll get the forms displayed in the chart below:

	SINGULAR	PLURAL
FIRST PERSON	ἀναγιγνώσκω	ἀναγιγνώσκομεν
SECOND PERSON	ἀναγιγνώσκεις	ἀναγιγνώσκετε
THIRD PERSON	ἀναγιγνώσκει	ἀναγιγνώσκουσι(ν)

Here's an example sentence with ἀναγιγνώσκω.

ὁ φιλόσοφος πολλάκις ἀναγιγνώσκει. *(The philosopher reads often.)*

128

EXERCISES

1. ἐγὼ σπανίως ἀναγιγνώσκω.

2. οὔποτε ἀναγιγνώσκω ὅτι αἴλουρός εἰμι.

3. οἱ φιλόσοφοι πολλάκις ἀναγιγνώσκουσιν.

4. ὁ φιλόσοφος πολλάκις ἀναγιγνώσκει.

5. οὐ τρέχω.

6. ἡμεῖς πολλάκις γράφομεν ὅτι ἔμποροί ἐσμεν.

7. οἱ ἵπποι σπανίως τρέχουσιν.

8. πολλάκις καθεύδομεν ὅτι ἐσμὲν αἴλουροι.

9. ὁ στρατηγὸς σπανίως καθεύδει.

10. ἐσμὲν ἔμποροι.

Answers on page 239.

LESSON 98

A SUBJECT WITH TWO VERBS

Sometimes in an English sentence, the subject will have two verbs. Here's an example of what I mean:

The teachers are reading and writing.

In that sentence, the word *teachers* is the subject. But the teachers aren't just doing one thing—they are reading *and* writing. So the sentence has one subject and two verbs.

Sometimes you'll see that same kind of thing in ancient Greek. Here's that same sentence shown above, but in Greek.

οἱ διδάσκαλοι ἀναγιγνώσκουσι καὶ γράφουσιν. *(The teachers are reading and writing.)*

You could translate the sentence as *The teachers are reading and they are writing.* But there is really no need to put the pronoun *they* in your translation—you can just leave it out and translate the sentence as *The teachers are reading and writing.*

EXERCISES

1. οἱ φιλόσοφοι ἀναγιγνώσκουσι καὶ γράφουσιν.

2. ὁ διδάσκαλος γράφει καὶ ἀναγιγνώσκει.

3. ὁ ἔμπορος καὶ ὁ γεωργὸς τρέχουσιν.

4. Κάδμος ἐστὶν ἵππος.

5. ὁ ἰᾱτρὸς ἀναγιγνώσκει καὶ γράφει.

6. σπανίως καθεύδετε ὅτι γεωργοί ἐστε.

7. Ἀλέξανδρός ἐστι φιλόσοφος καὶ διδάσκαλος.

8. ὑμεῖς ἐστε στρατηγοί.

9. σπανίως γράφετε καὶ ἀναγιγνώσκετε.

10. ὁ φιλόσοφος οὐκ ἔστιν ἰᾱτρός.

Answers on page 239.

130

LESSON 99

NEW WORD   *νῦν*

MEANING   *now*

PRONUNCIATION TIP: Remember to round your lips when you pronounce the letter *upsilon*.

Here's an example sentence with our new word for this lesson:

οἱ διδάσκαλοι νῦν γράφουσιν.   *(The teachers are writing now.)*

EXERCISES

1. ἡμεῖς νῦν γράφομεν.

2. νῦν ἀναγιγνώσκουσιν οἱ φιλόσοφοι.

3. νῦν ἀναγιγνώσκομεν καὶ γράφομεν ὅτι διδάσκαλοί ἐσμεν.

4. σπανίως καθεύδει ὁ ἔμπορος.

5. Κάδμος καὶ Τηλέμαχος καθεύδουσιν.

6. πολλάκις γράφει ὁ διδάσκαλος.

7. τρέχουσιν ὁ ἵππος καὶ ὁ αἴλουρος.

8. σὺ οὐκ εἶ ἰᾱτρός.

9. οἱ φιλόσοφοι οὐκ εἰσὶν ἰᾱτροί.

10. γεωργός εἰμι.

Answers on page 239.

131

LESSON 100

NEW WORD   καθ᾽ ἡμέρᾱν

MEANING   *daily, every day*

PRONUNCIATION TIP: This phrase sounds like *kath-heh-MEH-rahn*.

Our new word for this lesson is really two words, but they are joined together in a special way. First we have the word κατά which can mean several different things such as *down, according to,* and *by.* Then we have the word ἡμέρᾱ which means *day.* Together, these two words form an expression that means *daily* or *every day.*

When you put these two words together, something special happens called *elision.* It's kind of a long story, but sometimes, when there is a vowel at the end of one word and another vowel at the beginning of the next word, the first vowel can go away. The apostrophe is there where the vowel used to be. Other spelling changes can happen too—that's why the letter *tau* in κατά changes into a *theta.* This is the same kind of spelling change that we saw before when the word οὐκ turned into οὐχ before a rough breathing. In this beginning book you will only see these spelling changes in a couple of words, but it is still a good idea to understand how and why the change is happening.

EXERCISES

1. οἱ αἴλουροι καθ᾽ ἡμέρᾱν καθεύδουσιν.

2. καθ᾽ ἡμέρᾱν ἀναγιγνώσκω ὅτι φιλόσοφός εἰμι.

3. ἡμεῖς καθ᾽ ἡμέρᾱν ἀναγιγνώσκομεν καὶ γράφομεν ὅτι διδάσκαλοί ἐσμεν.

4. νῦν καθεύδομεν.

5. σπανίως καθεύδουσιν οἱ γεωργοί.

6. ὁ γεωργός ἐστι στρατηγός.

7. πολλάκις τρέχουσιν οἱ ἵπποι.

8. Τηλέμαχος πολλάκις ἀναγιγνώσκει ὅτι διδάσκαλός ἐστιν.

9. ἐγὼ καθ' ἡμέρᾱν τρέχω.

10. οἱ ἔμποροι οὐκ εἰσὶ γεωργοί.

Answers on page 239.

LESSON 101

DIRECT OBJECTS

A direct object is a noun that is the target of the action being performed by the subject of the sentence. Here is an example:

Harold plays the drums.

In this sentence, the word *drums* is the direct object. Here is another example:

Helen ate the orange.

In this sentence, the word *orange* is the direct object. See if you can find the direct object in each of the exercises below:

EXERCISES

1. Mr. Jones bought a newspaper.
2. I will see a movie tomorrow.
3. Harry is playing the trombone.
4. On Saturday, we will play baseball.
5. James caught a fish.
6. They accidentally broke the radio.
7. Y'all painted the wrong building.
8. Yesterday we listened to a long speech.
9. Mr. Underwood lost his wallet.
10. Geraldine saw a deer in the woods.

Answers on page 240.

LESSON 102

THE PREDICATE NOMINATIVE

In the last lesson, you learned that a direct object is the target of the action. For example, in the following sentence the word *dog* is the direct object.

Fred chased the dog.

But what if the verb is not an action verb? What if the verb is a verb of being or existing, as in this example:

Fred is a dog.

In that sentence, the word *dog* is not a direct object. Why? Because only an action verb can generate a direct object. The verb in that sentence is the word *is*, which is a verb of being. The dog is not the target of any action—instead, Fred is just being a dog. When you use a verb of being to make a "this is that" kind of sentence, the "that" word is not a direct object—instead, it is called a *predicate nominative*. Therefore in the sentence above, the word *dog* is a predicate nominative. Many of the Greek exercises that you have translated so far in this book have contained predicate nominatives.

In each of the following exercises the word *dog* is either a direct object or a predicate nominative. See if you can figure out which one it is.

EXERCISES

1. Fluffy is our dog.
2. The cat chased the dog.
3. We saw the dog.
4. Did you feed the dog?
5. The kids are all petting the dog.
6. A golden retriever is a dog.
7. Yesterday we bathed the dog.
8. The vet examined the dog.
9. Rex was our dog.
10. My best friend is a dog.

Answers on page 240.

LESSON 103

DIRECT OBJECTS (THIS TIME IN GREEK)

As I mentioned before, a Greek noun changes depending on the role it plays or the function it performs in a sentence.

When ὁ γεωργός is the subject of a sentence, it keeps its same article and spelling. But when ὁ γεωργός is the direct object in a sentence, a couple of things happen. First, the article changes to τόν. Also the ending of the noun changes from -ος to -ον. That gives us τὸν γεωργόν.

Let's work through some examples using the word *farmer* so we can observe the different forms of ὁ γεωργός in actual sentences.

In this first sentence, let's use the word *farmer* as the subject of a sentence.

ὁ γεωργός has a horse.

In that sentence, the farmer is the subject of the sentence, so the article stays as ὁ and the ending stays as -ος, leaving us with ὁ γεωργός. So far so good.

Next, let's use the word *farmer* as the direct object in a sentence.

I see τὸν γεωργόν.

In that sentence, the word *farmer* is the direct object, so the article changes to τόν and the ending of the noun changed to -ον to make τὸν γεωργόν.

Pay close attention to this last example, in which the verb is a verb of being, not an action verb.

That man is ὁ γεωργός.

In that sentence, the word *farmer* is not a direct object. A direct object can only happen after an action verb, not a verb of being. Instead, the word *farmer* in that sentence is a predicate nominative, so the article stays as ὁ and the ending remains as -ος.

In the exercises below, choose as your answer either ὁ γεωργός or τὸν γεωργόν. Then, give the reason for your choice. Choose from among the following three reasons:

- Because it is the subject of the sentence
- Because it is the direct object of the sentence
- Because it is a predicate nominative

Write your answers in your notebook or on a separate sheet of paper.

EXERCISES

1. ὁ γεωργός / τὸν γεωργόν is plowing the field.

2. I am ὁ γεωργός / τὸν γεωργόν.

3. I saw ὁ γεωργός / τὸν γεωργόν running toward the barn.

4. ὁ γεωργός / τὸν γεωργόν is fixing his tractor.

5. The man greeted ὁ γεωργός / τὸν γεωργόν.

6. Someday, Jimmy will be ὁ γεωργός / τὸν γεωργόν.

7. ὁ γεωργός / τὸν γεωργόν is harvesting the corn.

Answers on page 240.

LESSON 104

NEW WORD ἔχω

MEANING *I have*

PRONUNCIATION TIP: Remember that the letter *chi* represents a gentle scraping sound in the back of the mouth.

Our new word for this lesson is the verb ἔχω. It means *I have*. The stem is ἐχ- so if you add the personal endings to the stem, you'll get the forms in the chart below:

	SINGULAR	PLURAL
FIRST PERSON	ἔχω	ἔχομεν
SECOND PERSON	ἔχεις	ἔχετε
THIRD PERSON	ἔχει	ἔχουσι(ν)

You've been learning about direct objects for the past couple of lessons—now it's time to put that knowledge to good use as we start to work with Greek sentences that have a direct object. We can make that kind of sentence by using the word ἔχω, our new verb for this lesson.

Let's get started with some example sentences that have ἔχω along with a direct object. Remember that the ending of a direct object will be -ον and the definite article (if it has one) will be τόν.

- ἔχω τὸν ἵππον. *(I have the horse.)*
- Κάδμος τὸν αἴλουρον ἔχει. *(Cadmus has the cat.)*

137

- οὐκ ἔχομεν ἵππον. (We do not have a horse.)

In these exercises, watch for the new verb ἔχω along with a direct object.

EXERCISES

1. ἔχω αἴλουρον.

2. εἰμὶ αἴλουρος.

3. ἔχεις τὸν ἵππον.

4. σὺ οὐκ εἶ ἵππος.

5. Κάδμος ἔχει ἵππον ὅτι γεωργός ἐστιν.

6. τὸν ἵππον οὐκ ἔχετε.

7. τὸν αἴλουρον νῦν ἔχομεν.

8. ἐγὼ πολλάκις καθεύδω ὅτι αἴλουρός εἰμι.

9. Ἀλέξανδρος σπανίως ἀναγιγνώσκει καὶ γράφει.

10. καθ᾽ ἡμέρᾱν γράφουσιν οἱ φιλόσοφοι.

Answers on page 240.

LESSON 105

NEW WORD   χοῖρος

MEANING   *pig*

PRONUNCIATION TIP: This word contains the οι diphthong which sounds like the vowel sound in words such as *oil*, *soil*, and *toil*.

It's time to "ham it up" with our new word for this lesson. Now we can make sentences in which the farmer has other animals besides just horses (and an occasional lazy cat).

Remember that if χοῖρος is a direct object, the ending will change to -ον and the definite article (if it has one) will be τόν, as seen in this example sentence:

ὁ γεωργὸς τὸν χοῖρον ἔχει. (*The farmer has the pig.*)

EXERCISES

1. ὁ χοῖρος τρέχει.

2. τὸν χοῖρον ἔχω.

3. οἱ χοῖροι νῦν καθεύδουσιν.

4. Κάδμος χοῖρον καὶ ἵππον ἔχει ὅτι γεωργός ἐστιν.

5. οἱ χοῖροι τρέχουσιν.

6. οὔποτε ἀναγιγνώσκομεν ὅτι χοῖροι ἐσμέν.

7. σπανίως γράφει ὁ στρατηγός.

8. οἱ διδάσκαλοι σπανίως καθεύδουσιν.

9. ὁ ἔμπορος πολλάκις καθεύδει.

10. ἡμεῖς καθ' ἡμέραν γράφομεν καὶ ἀναγιγνώσκομεν.

Answers on page 240.

LESSON 106

NEW WORD   κάλαμος

MEANING   *pen*

The Greek word κάλαμος means a *reed*, like the kind of small bamboo reed that grows in marshy areas. In the ancient world they would take a reed, sharpen it at one end, dip it in ink, and write with it. Therefore the word κάλαμος also means *reed-pen*. And that's how we will use the word κάλαμος in this book—as a pen for writing.

EXERCISES

1. κάλαμον ἔχω.

2. ὁ γεωργὸς οὐκ ἔχει κάλαμον.

3. ὁ φιλόσοφος κάλαμον ἔχει ὅτι καθ᾽ ἡμέρᾱν γράφει.

4. οἱ γεωργοὶ σπανίως γράφουσιν.

5. οὐκ ἔχω αἴλουρον ὅτι γεωργὸς οὐκ εἰμί.

6. πολλάκις τρέχουσιν οἱ χοῖροι.

7. οἱ διδάσκαλοι καθ᾽ ἡμέρᾱν ἀναγιγνώσκουσιν.

8. οἱ ἵπποι οὔποτε καθεύδουσιν.

9. τρέχει ὁ ἔμπορος.

10. νῦν χοῖρον ἔχω.

Answers on page 240.

140

LESSON 107

NEW WORD   διώκω

MEANING   *I chase*

This new verb, which means *chase*, will help you to practice working with direct objects. Get ready for some silly sentences with people (or animals) chasing each other!

The stem of this new verb is διωκ- so if you add the personal endings to the stem, you'll get the forms in the chart below:

	SINGULAR	PLURAL
FIRST PERSON	διώκω	διώκομεν
SECOND PERSON	διώκεις	διώκετε
THIRD PERSON	διώκει	διώκουσι(ν)

Here's an example sentence with this new verb:

ὁ γεωργὸς διώκει τὸν ἵππον. *(The farmer is chasing the horse.)*

EXERCISES

1. οἱ γεωργοὶ τὸν χοῖρον διώκουσιν.

2. ὁ χοῖρος Τηλέμαχον νῦν διώκει.

3. καθ᾽ ἡμέρᾱν τὸν αἴλουρον διώκεις.

141

4. ἡμεῖς τὸν αἴλουρον οὔποτε διώκομεν.

5. Κάδμος ἔχει κάλαμον ὅτι διδάσκαλός ἐστιν.

6. Ἀλέξανδρος διώκει Τηλέμαχον.

7. οἱ ἵπποι καὶ οἱ χοῖροι τὸν γεωργὸν διώκουσιν.

8. οὐκ ἔχω ἵππον ὅτι οὐκ εἰμὶ γεωργός.

9. Τηλέμαχος καὶ Κάδμος σπανίως ἀναγιγνώσκουσι καὶ γράφουσιν ὅτι διδάσκαλοι οὐκ εἰσίν.

10. πολλάκις καθεύδομεν ὅτι αἴλουροί ἐσμεν.

Answers on page 241.

LESSON 108

NOUNS AND ACCENTS

In this book I have tried not to overwhelm you with too much information about Greek accents and all the rules that go with them. But now, since you are beginning to learn about the different noun endings, I need to tell you another thing or two about accents and the way they behave with nouns.

Recently you have been learning about the various endings that nouns can have. For example, γεωργός is singular, so it has the ending -ος. When it is plural, the ending changes to -οι and so it becomes γεωργοί. And, as you recently learned, when it is the direct object, the ending changes to -ον and it becomes γεωργόν. So that's three different noun endings so far, with many more to come.

Here is the new thing I need to tell you: the different endings of a noun can affect the placement of the accent for that particular noun. It's a long story, but here is the basic idea: If a noun ending contains a long vowel or a diphthong, it can cause the accent for that particular noun to move or change. In certain situations, it can cause the accent to move one syllable to the right. In other situations, it can cause an acute accent to change to a circumflex accent. Just in case you forgot, the acute accent is the one that points upward, and the circumflex is the one that looks like an upside down *u* or a wavy line, depending on the font.

In the next lesson we will examine this issue in more detail. For now, just understand that the final syllable of a noun (that is, its ending) can cause changes to the accent for that noun. And, just for review, here are the names of the different kinds of Greek accents again in a handy chart.

ANCIENT GREEK ACCENTS

ACUTE	$\acute{\alpha}$
GRAVE	$\grave{\alpha}$
CIRCUMFLEX	$\hat{\alpha}$ or $\tilde{\alpha}$

LESSON 109

LONG VOWELS AND DIPHTHONGS IN NOUN ENDINGS

In the last lesson you learned that the accent of a noun can change when the ending of the noun contains a long vowel or diphthong. In this lesson, let's take a look at some of the specific vowels and diphthongs that we might see in the endings of masculine nouns.

Let's look at the vowels first. Near the beginning of this book we collected the various vowels into a handy chart. Here's that chart again, just for review.

ANCIENT GREEK VOWEL LENGTHS		
ALWAYS SHORT	ϵ *epsilon*	o *omicron*
ALWAYS LONG	η *eta*	ω *omega*
COULD BE LONG OR SHORT	α *alpha*	ι *iota* υ *upsilon*

Epsilon and *omicron* are always short. *Alpha, iota,* and *upsilon* can be either long or short. *Eta* and *omega* are always long.

With the masculine nouns we are working with, a couple of the endings will contain an *omega*. An *omega* is always long, so if you see an *omega* in a noun ending, that ending can cause the noun's accent to move or change.

A couple of noun endings will contain an *omicron* or an *epsilon*. Since these vowels are short, they will not cause the accent to move or change. For example, in the word διδάσκαλος the ending is -ος. Since that ending contains an *omicron*, which is a short vowel, it will not affect the accent.

144

Now let's take a look at diphthongs. In ancient Greek, a diphthong is considered to be long, like a long vowel such as *eta* or *omega*. So, if a noun ending contains a diphthong, that ending can affect the accent of the noun. For the masculine nouns we are studying, you will see these two diphthongs in the endings:

$$οι \quad ου$$

So if you see a noun ending with one of those diphthongs in it, that ending can cause the accent to move or change.

There is, however, one exception that you should know about. In the plural form you know, the οι diphthong does not count as long, and so will not affect the accent. For example, the word διδάσκαλοι *(teachers)* has the οι diphthong as its ending—but in this particular form it won't affect the accent. This is an exception to the rule. But in other endings that you will learn later, the οι diphthong will affect the accent.

LESSON 110

PLURAL DIRECT OBJECTS

So far we have only been working with singular direct objects. For example, if Cadmus has one horse, we could make a sentence like this one:

Κάδμος τὸν ἵππον ἔχει. *(Cadmus has the horse.)*

In that example sentence, the horse is a singular direct object. Its ending is -ον and its article is τόν. But what if Cadmus has more than one horse? In that case, there is a different ending for the noun and a different article, too.

If the direct object is plural, the ending changes to -ους and the article changes to τούς, like this:

Κάδμος τοὺς ἵππους ἔχει. *(Cadmus has the horses.)*

Notice that the new noun ending you are learning in this lesson contains the ου diphthong. Over the past couple of lessons, I have been telling you that when a noun ending contains a long vowel or a diphthong, it can cause the accent to move or change. So, let's take a look at how this long final syllable will affect the accent in the nouns you know so far.

For a noun that has its accent on the last syllable, this long final syllable will not change anything. Take, for example, the noun στρατηγός. If we change the ending to -ους, the accent stays at the end, like this:

στρατηγός ⟶ στρατηγούς

Also, if there is an acute accent (that's the one that points upward) on the next-to-last syllable, the -ους ending won't change anything. You'll see this in words such as ἵππος.

ἵππος ⟶ ἵππους

146

But here's a situation in which the accent will change—if the noun has an acute accent on the third syllable from the end, a long final syllable will cause the accent to move one syllable to the right (toward the end of the word). An example of a word like this would be the word διδάσκαλος. Let's see what happens when we change the ending to -ους :

$$\delta\iota\delta\acute{\alpha}\sigma\kappa\alpha\lambda\text{ος} \longrightarrow \delta\iota\delta\alpha\sigma\kappa\acute{\alpha}\lambda\text{ους}$$

Notice that now the accent is no longer on the third syllable from the end—now it has moved one notch to the right. So when you see this form you'll have to make sure to pronounce it like *di-dah-SKAH-loose*, with the accent on the next to last syllable.

One last thing to mention—if a noun has a circumflex on the next-to-last syllable, a long final syllable will cause that accent to change to an acute accent. You only know one word like this, and that's the word χοῖρος. Here is what will happen when you change the ending to -ους.

$$\chi\text{οῖρος} \longrightarrow \chi\text{οίρους}$$

Not a huge change, but nevertheless something to be aware of.

Here are a few more example sentences to study before you try the exercises. Don't be surprised if the plural direct object forms have an accent that has moved from where you are used to seeing it!

- ὁ γεωργὸς οὐκ ἔχει αἰλούρους. *(The farmer does not have cats.)*
- ὁ γεωργὸς τοὺς ἵππους πολλάκις διώκει. *(The farmer often chases the horses.)*
- οἱ διδάσκαλοι καλάμους ἔχουσιν ὅτι καθ᾽ ἡμέρᾱν γράφουσιν. *(The teachers have pens because they write daily.)*

EXERCISES

1. ὁ γεωργὸς ἔχει ἵππον.

2. ὁ γεωργὸς ἔχει ἵππους.

3. ὁ γεωργὸς ἔχει τὸν ἵππον.

4. ὁ γεωργὸς ἔχει τοὺς ἵππους.

5. ὁ αἴλουρος τοὺς χοίρους καθ’ ἡμέρᾱν διώκει.

6. ὁ φιλόσοφος ἔχει τοὺς καλάμους.

7. ἐγὼ ἵππους οὐκ ἔχω ὅτι γεωργὸς οὐκ εἰμί.

8. οἱ στρατηγοὶ οὐκ ἔχουσιν ἵππους.

9. σπανίως ἀναγιγνώσκομεν.

10. Τηλέμαχος τοὺς χοίρους νῦν διώκει.

Answers on page 241.

LESSON 111

NEW WORD *ἀγοράζω*

MEANING *I buy*

PRONUNCIATION TIP: The letter *zeta* sounds like the *sd* in the word *wisdom*. So our new word for this lesson sounds like *ah-goh-RAHZ-doe.*

In an ancient Greek city, the *agora* (pronounced *ah-goh-RAH*) was a public area similar to a town square where people could get together, do some shopping, or hear speeches. Our new word for this lesson is a verb related to the word *agora*. The verb *ἀγοράζω* can mean to hang around in the *agora,* or it can simply mean to buy something. In this book, we will use it to mean *buy*.

	SINGULAR	PLURAL
FIRST PERSON	ἀγοράζω	ἀγοράζομεν
SECOND PERSON	ἀγοράζεις	ἀγοράζετε
THIRD PERSON	ἀγοράζει	ἀγοράζουσι(ν)

Here's an example sentence with our new word for this lesson:

Κάδμος ἵππους πολλάκις ἀγοράζει. *(Cadmus buys horses often.)*

149

1. οἱ ἔμποροι χοίρους ἀγοράζουσιν.

2. οὔποτε ἀγοράζομεν ἵππους ὅτι οὐκ ἐσμὲν γεωργοί.

3. ὁ φιλόσοφος τοὺς καλάμους ἀγοράζει.

4. ὁ ἔμπορος τὸν χοῖρον διώκει.

5. Ἀλέξανδρος καθ' ἡμέρᾱν ἀναγιγνώσκει ὅτι φιλόσοφός ἐστιν.

6. ὑμεῖς ἔχετε καλάμους ὅτι φιλόσοφοί ἐστε.

7. ὁ διδάσκαλος νῦν γράφει καὶ ἀναγιγνώσκει.

8. Τηλέμαχος Ἀλέξανδρον διώκει.

9. ἐγὼ καθ' ἡμέρᾱν ἀγοράζω καλάμους ὅτι διδάσκαλός εἰμι.

10. Κάδμος καθεύδει.

Answers on page 241.

LESSON 112

NEW WORD   *ἄρτος*

MEANING   *bread*

No more loafing around! Get to work on our new word for this lesson which means *bread*. Here's an example sentence:

Ἀλέξανδρος καθ' ἡμέρᾱν ἀγοράζει ἄρτον. *(Alexander buys bread every day.)*

EXERCISES

1. Κάδμος τὸν ἄρτον ἔχει.

2. ἄρτον ἔχομεν ὅτι γεωργοί ἐσμεν.

3. οἱ φιλόσοφοι ἄρτον σπανίως ἀγοράζουσιν.

4. οἱ αἴλουροι καθεύδουσιν.

5. ὁ ἰᾱτρὸς τὸν γεωργὸν διώκει.

6. οἱ διδάσκαλοι καλάμους πολλάκις ἀγοράζουσιν.

7. οὐκ ἔχω ἵππους ὅτι οὐκ εἰμὶ γεωργός.

8. ὁ ἔμπορος πολλάκις χοίρους ἀγοράζει.

9. ἡμεῖς διώκομεν τοὺς χοίρους.

10. σπανίως γράφω ὅτι οὐκ ἔχω κάλαμον.

Answers on page 241.

LESSON 113

NEW WORD   πάντοτε

MEANING   *always*

PRONUNCIATION TIP: This three-syllable word has the stress on the first syllable. It sounds like *PAHN-toe-teh*.

Our new word for this lesson, like many Greek words, is a combination of two smaller words. The πάν- part of the word means *all* or *every*. We see this word at the beginning of English words such as *panorama*, *pandemic*, and *pantheon*. The -τότε part of the word means *at that time* or *then* (even though it's not spelled the same, it is related to the -ποτε part of the word οὔποτε). So πάντοτε literally means *at every time*, that is, *always*.

Here's an example sentence with πάντοτε.

> πάντοτε ἄρτον ἔχομεν ὅτι γεωργοί ἐσμεν. (*We always have bread because we are farmers.*)

EXERCISES

1. οἱ αἴλουροι πάντοτε καθεύδουσιν.

2. οἱ διδάσκαλοι πάντοτε καλάμους ἔχουσιν ὅτι καθ' ἡμέρᾱν γράφουσιν.

3. Τηλέμαχος ἵππους πάντοτε ἔχει ὅτι γεωργός ἐστιν.

4. οὔποτε ἀγοράζομεν χοίρους ὅτι οὐκ ἐσμὲν ἔμποροι.

5. ὁ χοῖρος τοὺς αἰλούρους διώκει.

6. πολλάκις καθεύδομεν ὅτι ἐσμὲν αἴλουροι.

7. οἱ ἔμποροι τὸν ἰᾱτρὸν διώκουσιν.

152

8. καθεύδουσιν οἱ αἴλουροι.

9. ὑμεῖς οὐκ ἔχετε ἄρτον.

10. οὔποτε ἀναγιγνώσκομεν ὅτι οὐκ ἐσμὲν φιλόσοφοι.

Answers on page 241.

LESSON 114

NEW WORD   ἐσθίω

MEANING   *I eat*

PRONUNCIATION TIP: Notice that for each of the six present tense forms of this verb, the stress is on the second syllable. For example ἐσθίω sounds like *ess-THEE-oh*.

See if you can digest our new word for this lesson. The stem of this verb is ἐσθί- so if you add the personal endings to the stem, you'll get the forms shown in the chart below:

	SINGULAR	PLURAL
FIRST PERSON	ἐσθίω	ἐσθίομεν
SECOND PERSON	ἐσθίεις	ἐσθίετε
THIRD PERSON	ἐσθίει	ἐσθίουσι(ν)

Here's an example sentence for you to chew on:

$$\text{ἄρτον καθ' ἡμέρᾱν ἐσθίομεν.} \quad \textit{(We eat bread every day.)}$$

EXERCISES

1. ἐγὼ ἄρτον οὔποτε ἐσθίω.

2. Κάδμος ἄρτον σπανίως ἐσθίει.

3. καθ' ἡμέρᾱν ἀγοράζω καὶ ἐσθίω ἄρτον.

4. πάντοτε ἐσθίετε ἄρτον.

5. οἱ γεωργοὶ ἵππους ἔχουσιν.

6. ὁ αἴλουρος τοὺς χοίρους διώκει.

7. Ἀλέξανδρος αἴλουρον οὐκ ἔχει.

8. ὁ γεωργὸς ἔχει τοὺς ἵππους καὶ τοὺς χοίρους.

9. κάλαμον νῦν ἀγοράζομεν.

10. πολλάκις ἀγοράζω ἵππους ὅτι ἔμπορός εἰμι.

Answers on page 241.

LESSON 115

NEW WORD   μάγειρος

MEANING   *cook*

PRONUNCIATION TIP: The stress is on the first syllable, so it sounds something like *MAH-gei-rohs.*

Our new word for this lesson is the Greek word for a cook, as in someone who prepares food. Here's an example sentence:

οἱ μάγειροι τὸν ἄρτον ἀγοράζουσιν.   *(The cooks are buying the bread.)*

EXERCISES

1. οἱ μάγειροι χοῖρον οὐκ ἔχουσιν.

2. Κάδμος μάγειρός ἐστιν.

3. ὁ μάγειρος χοίρους πολλάκις ἀγοράζει.

4. Τηλέμαχος τὸν χοῖρον διώκει ὅτι μάγειρός ἐστιν.

5. οἱ ἵπποι νῦν καθεύδουσιν.

6. ὑμεῖς σπανίως τρέχετε ὅτι στρατηγοί ἐστε.

7. πολλάκις ἐσθίω ἄρτον.

8. Ἀλέξανδρος οὐκ ἔστιν ἰᾱτρός.

9. οὐκ ἔχω κάλαμον.

10. πάντοτε καθεύδομεν ὅτι αἴλουροί ἐσμεν.

Answers on page 242.

155

LESSON 116

CASES

In ancient Greek, a noun's ending changes depending on the role or function that particular noun is performing in the sentence. In grammatical terms, we call these different functions or roles *cases*. When we use a noun as the subject of a sentence, that noun is said to be in the *nominative case*. We also use the nominative case for predicate nominatives. When we use a noun as a direct object, that noun is said to be in the *accusative case*. In ancient Greek, there are five cases. As you can see in the following chart, you already know two out of the five cases. You'll learn the other three cases in upcoming lessons.

	SINGULAR	PLURAL
NOMINATIVE (SUBJ./PRED. NOM.)	ὁ γεωργός	οἱ γεωργοί
ACCUSATIVE (DIRECT OBJECT)	τὸν γεωργόν	τοὺς γεωργούς

Each case performs certain functions while working together with the other cases to create meaningful sentences. As you learn the remaining cases, you will be able to translate more complex (and interesting) sentences.

From now on when we study a particular noun, I will present it in a chart like the one seen above, along with the definite article for each noun. That way, you can easily study the various forms of each noun and review the definite articles, too.

LESSON 117

NEW WORD   χρῡσός

MEANING   *gold*

PRONUNCIATION TIP: Notice that the *upsilon* in χρῡσός has a macron, indicating that it is a long *upsilon*. Remember to keep your lips rounded as you pronounce the *upsilon*—and put the stress on the second syllable of the word.

In the last lesson I introduced you to the idea of noun cases. You learned that when a noun is the subject of the sentence, it is in the nominative case, and when it is the direct object it is in the accusative case.

As I mentioned before, whenever I introduce a new noun to you, I will include a chart so you can see all the different forms of the noun, along with the definite articles. Of course, you don't know all the cases yet—but here are the ones you know so far:

	SINGULAR	PLURAL
NOMINATIVE (SUBJ./PRED. NOM.)	ὁ χρῡσός	οἱ χρῡσοί
ACCUSATIVE (DIRECT OBJECT)	τὸν χρῡσόν	τοὺς χρῡσούς

157

Here's an example sentence with our new word for this lesson:

ὁ Κάδμος χρῡσὸν ἔχει ὅτι ἔμπορός ἐστιν. *(Cadmus has gold because he is a merchant.)*

EXERCISES

1. οἱ φιλόσοφοι οὔποτε χρῡσὸν ἔχουσιν.

2. ἐγὼ χρῡσὸν σπανίως ἔχω ὅτι γεωργός εἰμι.

3. οἱ ἔμποροι χρῡσὸν πάντοτε ἔχουσιν.

4. οἱ μάγειροι τοὺς χοίρους διώκουσιν.

5. σὺ οὔποτε ἀγοράζεις καλάμους ὅτι οὔποτε γράφεις.

6. κάλαμον ἔχω ὅτι καθ' ἡμέρᾱν γράφω.

7. οἱ ἵπποι νῦν καθεύδουσιν.

8. ὑμεῖς ἔμποροί ἐστε.

9. καθ' ἡμέρᾱν ἀναγιγνώσκεις καὶ γράφεις ὅτι ἰᾱτρὸς εἶ.

10. πάντοτε ἐσθίω τὸν ἄρτον.

Answers on page 242.

LESSON 118

NEW WORD   τῡρός

MEANING   *cheese*

PRONUNCIATION TIP: The macron over the letter *upsilon* shows that it is a long vowel. Don't forget to round your lips when you pronounce it. Also, notice that the stress is on the second syllable of the word.

I hope you're not lactose intolerant, because this lesson is going to be a cheesy one. Here are the different forms of τῡρός, our new word for this lesson.

	Singular	Plural
Nominative (subj./pred. nom.)	ὁ τῡρός	οἱ τῡροί
Accusative (direct object)	τὸν τῡρόν	τοὺς τῡρούς

The word τῡρός is related to our English word *butter*. The ancient Greek word for *cow* is βοῦς (rhymes with *moose* and *goose*). When combined with the word τῡρός, you get the ancient Greek word βούτῡρος *(BOO-too-rohs)* which means *butter*.

In fact, since you know the word for *butter* now, let's put that word in the exercises too. After all, two words are "butter" than one. Here's an example sentence with both of our new words:

καθ' ἡμέρᾱν ἀγοράζει ὁ μάγειρος τῡρὸν καὶ
βούτῡρον. *(The cook buys cheese and butter every day.)*

EXERCISES

1. ὁ γεωργὸς πάντοτε βούτῡρον καὶ τῡρὸν ἔχει.

2. οὔποτε ἐσθίω τῡρόν.

3. πολλάκις ἐσθίω ἄρτον καὶ βούτῡρον.

4. Ἀλέξανδρος βούτῡρον οὔποτε ἀγοράζει ὅτι
γεωργός ἐστιν.

5. ὁ αἴλουρος τὸν τῡρὸν ἐσθίει.

6. οἱ μάγειροι Τηλέμαχον διώκουσιν ὅτι ἔχει τὸν
τῡρὸν καὶ τὸν ἄρτον.

7. τοὺς καλάμους οὐκ ἔχεις.

8. πάντοτε ἔχω χρῡσὸν ὅτι ἔμπορός εἰμι.

9. σὺ βούτῡρον καθ' ἡμέρᾱν ἀγοράζεις ὅτι εἶ μάγειρος.

10. νῦν καθεύδω.

Answers on page 242.

LESSON 119

NEW WORD ἄργυρος

MEANING *silver*

The South American country known as Argentina was given its name because it was supposed to be a land rich in silver. The word *Argentina* comes from the Latin word **argentum** which means *silver*. In science, the symbol for silver (element #47 on the periodic table) is **Ag** because it's simply an abbreviation of the Latin word **argentum**. The Greek word ἄργυρος, our new word for this lesson, is related to that Latin word, so it has a somewhat similar spelling—notice that they both start with *arg-*.

Here is a chart showing the different forms of ἄργυρος.

	Singular	Plural
Nominative (subj./pred. nom.)	ὁ ἄργυρος	οἱ ἄργυροι
Accusative (direct object)	τὸν ἄργυρον	τοὺς ἀργύρους

Here's an example sentence with our new word for this lesson.

ἡμεῖς ἄργυρον οὔποτε ἔχομεν ὅτι διδάσκαλοί ἐσμεν. *(We never have silver because we are teachers.)*

161

EXERCISES

1. οὐκ ἔχω ἄργυρον ὅτι φιλόσοφός εἰμι.

2. Τηλέμαχος καὶ Κάδμος τοὺς ἐμπόρους διώκουσιν ὅτι χρῦσὸν καὶ ἄργυρον ἔχουσιν.

3. ἔχω τὸν ἄργυρον.

4. ὁ μάγειρος διώκει τὸν χοῖρον.

5. οἱ στρατηγοὶ χρῦσὸν καὶ ἄργυρον ἔχουσιν.

6. αἴλουροί ἐστε.

7. ἡμεῖς βούτῦρον σπανίως ἐσθίομεν ὅτι οὐκ ἐσμὲν γεωργοί.

8. Τηλέμαχος πάντοτε ἔχει χρῦσὸν ὅτι ἔμπορός ἐστιν.

9. τῦρὸν καὶ βούτῦρον καθ᾽ ἡμέρᾱν ἀγοράζομεν.

10. σπανίως καθεύδω ὅτι εἰμὶ γεωργός.

Answers on page 242.

LESSON 120

POSSESSION

In English, we often show possession by using an apostrophe followed by the letter *s*. Observe the following examples:

> Fred's car
>
> The nation's flag
>
> Arizona's capital

Another way we show possession is by using the word *of*.

> The peak of the mountain
>
> The smell of garlic
>
> The beginning of the show

Therefore, in English, when you want to show possession of something, you must decide whether to use an apostrophe or the word *of*.

Here are a few of the most basic rules to remember when using apostrophes:

	RULE	EXAMPLE
RULE #1	To make a noun that does not end in *s* possessive, just add an apostrophe and an *s*.	Lauren always wants to borrow Kate's Greek book.
RULE #2	To make a singular noun that ends in *s* possessive, add an apostrophe and an *s* (just like rule #1).	The class's favorite subject was Greek.
RULE #3	To make a plural noun that ends in *s* possessive, add an apostrophe to the end of the word.	Due to increased interest in Greek, all the books' covers are starting to wear out.

LESSON 121

THE GENITIVE CASE

In Greek, the most common way to show possession is by using a noun case called the *genitive case.* In the chart, the genitive case is shown on the second row. The article for the genitive singular is τοῦ and the noun ending is -ου. So, for the noun γεωργός, the genitive singular form (with the definite article included) would be τοῦ γεωργοῦ.

	SINGULAR	PLURAL
NOMINATIVE (SUBJ./PRED. NOM.)	ὁ γεωργός	οἱ γεωργοί
GENITIVE (POSSESSION)	τοῦ γεωργοῦ	
ACCUSATIVE (DIRECT OBJECT)	τὸν γεωργόν	τοὺς γεωργούς

The phrase τοῦ γεωργοῦ is in the genitive case, so we could translate it as *of the farmer* or *the farmer's.* So if the farmer owns a horse, we could say this:

ὁ ἵππος τοῦ γεωργοῦ *(the horse of the farmer* OR *the farmer's horse)*

The word ἵππος is in the nominative case, and since the word γεωργοῦ is in the genitive case (along with the article τοῦ) it is possessing the horse. The noun in the genitive case will often come right after the noun it is possessing.

When you translate this phrase, you have two choices of how to do it. You could use the word *of* and say *The horse of the farmer.* Or, you could use an apostrophe and the letter *s* and say *The farmer's horse.* Try to use the translation that sounds

164

the most natural in each situation. For this particular example, saying *the farmer's horse* sounds more natural than saying the *horse of the farmer*.

Any noun in a sentence can be possessed by another noun in the genitive case. For example, the subject of a sentence can be possessed by another noun:

ὁ αἴλουρος τοῦ ἰᾱτροῦ ἔχει τὸν τῡρόν. *(The doctor's cat has the cheese.)*

A direct object can be possessed by a genitive noun too, like this:

τὸν κάλαμον τοῦ διδασκάλου ἔχω. *(I have the teacher's pen.)*

A person's name can be in the genitive case, like this:

ἔχομεν τὸν ἵππον Τηλεμάχου. *(We have Telemachus's horse.)*

As you translate, watch carefully for the endings of nouns. The ending of a noun will tell you what case the noun is, giving you a big clue about what that particular noun is doing in the sentence.

A quick note about accents: the -ου ending is a diphthong, so it can cause a noun's accent to move or change. For example, notice that in the genitive singular form διδασκάλου the accent is one syllable to the right of where it would be in the nominative singular. And, for the noun χοῖρος, notice that the genitive singular form χοίρου has an acute accent instead of a circumflex.

EXERCISES

1. ὁ αἴλουρος ἐσθίει τὸν ἄρτον τοῦ μαγείρου.

2. σὺ ἔχεις τὸν ἄργυρον Τηλεμάχου.

3. ὁ αἴλουρος τοῦ μαγείρου ἐσθίει τὸν τῡρόν.

4. διώκομεν τοὺς αἰλούρους Κάδμου.

5. πολλάκις βούτῡρον ἀγοράζω ὅτι μάγειρός εἰμι.

6. πάντοτε ἔχομεν καλάμους ὅτι διδάσκαλοί ἐσμεν.

7. ὁ μάγειρος τοὺς χοίρους πολλάκις διώκει.

8. οἱ ἵπποι Ἀλεξάνδρου πολλάκις τρέχουσιν.

9. Τηλέμαχος ἔχει χρῡσὸν καὶ ἄργυρον ὅτι ἔμπορός ἐστιν.

10. ὁ ἵππος τοῦ ἰᾱτροῦ τὸν βούτῡρον ἐσθίει.

Answers on page 242.

LESSON 122

NEW WORD   *υἱός*

MEANING   *son*

PRONUNCIATION TIP: This word starts out with the diphthong *υι* which sounds like the vowel sound in *queen*. It has a rough breathing and the stress on the second syllable, so it sounds something like *hwee-OHS*.

Here is a chart showing the forms that you have learned so far in this book.

	SINGULAR	PLURAL
NOMINATIVE (SUBJ./PRED. NOM.)	ὁ υἱός	οἱ υἱοί
GENITIVE (POSSESSION)	τοῦ υἱοῦ	
ACCUSATIVE (DIRECT OBJECT)	τὸν υἱόν	τοὺς υἱούς

Here are a couple of example sentences with *υἱός*.

- ὁ υἱὸς τοῦ γεωργοῦ ἵππον ἔχει. *(The farmer's son has a horse.)*
- οἱ χοῖροι τοὺς υἱοὺς Ἀλεξάνδρου διώκουσιν. *(The pigs are chasing Alexander's sons.)*

EXERCISES

1. Τηλέμαχος υἱὸν ἔχει.

2. οἱ υἱοὶ τοῦ γεωργοῦ τὸν χοῖρον διώκουσιν.

3. διώκομεν τοὺς υἱοὺς Κάδμου.

4. ὁ αἴλουρος τοῦ γεωργοῦ τὸν βούτῡρον ἐσθίει.

5. πάντοτε ἀναγιγνώσκομεν ὅτι φιλόσοφοί ἐσμεν.

6. οἱ μάγειροι τὸν χρῡσὸν ἔχουσιν.

7. ἐγὼ οὔποτε ἐσθίω τῡρόν.

8. οἱ ἵπποι τοῦ γεωργοῦ τρέχουσιν.

9. πάντοτε χρῡσὸν καὶ ἄργυρον ἔχετε ὅτι ἔμποροί ἐστε.

10. ὁ μάγειρος τὸν ἄρτον ἐσθίει.

Answers on page 243.

LESSON 123

THE GENITIVE PLURAL

Over the past few lessons you have learned how to translate the genitive case, but only in the singular—that is, when something is being possessed by only one person (or thing, or animal, etc.). But if something is being possessed by more than one person, you'll need the genitive plural.

In the genitive plural, the article changes to $\tau\hat{\omega}\nu$ and the ending of the noun changes to $-\omega\nu$. Therefore the genitive plural form of $\gamma\epsilon\omega\rho\gamma\delta\varsigma$ along with its article would be $\tau\hat{\omega}\nu\ \gamma\epsilon\omega\rho\gamma\hat{\omega}\nu$.

Here's how it fits into our chart:

	SINGULAR	PLURAL
NOMINATIVE (SUBJ./PRED. NOM.)	ὁ γεωργός	οἱ γεωργοί
GENITIVE (POSSESSION)	τοῦ γεωργοῦ	τῶν γεωργῶν
ACCUSATIVE (DIRECT OBJECT)	τὸν γεωργόν	τοὺς γεωργούς

Let's say, for example, that several farmers share ownership of a horse. We could make a phrase like this:

ὁ ἵππος τῶν γεωργῶν *(the horse of the farmers* OR *the farmers' horse)*

In this example, the horse is owned by more than one farmer, so the word for *farmer* was in the genitive plural.

168

And, as I have mentioned before, you have two choices of how you can translate this phrase. You could use the word *of* and say *the horse of the farmers*. Or, you could use an apostrophe and the letter *s* (of course, putting the apostrophe after the letter *s*) and say *the farmers' horse*. Either way is correct, but you should try to use the translation that sounds most natural in English. In this particular case, *the farmers' horse* sounds more natural. By the way, if you ever need to review the basic rules of apostrophes, you may refer back to lesson 120.

Here are a couple of example sentences to study before you try the exercises.

- οἱ υἱοὶ τῶν γεωργῶν τὸν χοῖρον διώκουσιν. *(The farmers' sons are chasing the pig.)*
- Τηλέμαχος ἔχει τὸν ἄργυρον τῶν ἐμπόρων. *(Telemachus has the merchants' silver.)*

A quick note about accents: the -ων ending contains the long vowel *omega*, so it can cause a noun's accent to move or change. For example, notice that the nominative singular διδάσκαλος has its accent three syllables from the end, but in the genitive plural form διδασκάλων the accent has moved one syllable over from that. And in the nominative singular χοῖρος, the accent is a circumflex, but in the genitive plural form χοίρων, the accent is an acute accent.

EXERCISES

1. οὔποτε ἐσθίομεν τὸν τῡρὸν τῶν γεωργῶν.

2. οἱ μάγειροι καθ' ἡμέρᾱν τὸν βούτῡρον τῶν γεωργῶν ἀγοράζουσιν.

3. οὐκ ἔχομεν τοὺς καλάμους τῶν διδασκάλων.

4. Ἀλέξανδρος ἔχει τὸν χρῡσὸν τῶν στρατηγῶν.

5. οὐκ ἔχομεν τὸν ἄργυρον τῶν ἐμπόρων.

6. οὐκ ἔχω τοὺς καλάμους τοῦ φιλοσόφου.

7. πολλάκις ἐσθίω ὅτι εἰμὶ χοῖρος.

169

8. Τηλέμαχος σπανίως γράφει ὅτι οὐκ ἔστι διδάσκαλος.

9. ὁ υἱὸς Ἀλεξάνδρου μάγειρός ἐστιν.

10. οἱ φιλόσοφοι πάντοτε ἀναγιγνώσκουσιν.

Answers on page 243.

LESSON 124

NEW WORD   ἀδελφός

MEANING   *brother*

Philadelphia is known as the city of brotherly love. In fact, that's the literal meaning of the word *Philadelphia*. The *phil-* part means *love* (you've already seen that root word in the word φιλόσοφος). The *-adelphia* part is related to our new word for this lesson which means *brother* or *brotherly*. Therefore the word *Philadelphia* really does mean *brotherly love*.

Here is a chart showing the different forms of ἀδελφός.

	SINGULAR	PLURAL
NOMINATIVE (SUBJ./PRED. NOM.)	ὁ ἀδελφός	οἱ ἀδελφοί
GENITIVE (POSSESSION)	τοῦ ἀδελφοῦ	τῶν ἀδελφῶν
ACCUSATIVE (DIRECT OBJECT)	τὸν ἀδελφόν	τοὺς ἀδελφούς

And here is an example sentence using our new word:

$$\text{ὁ ἀδελφός Ἀλεξάνδρου οὐκ ἔχει αἴλουρον.}$$
(Alexander's brother does not have a cat.)

EXERCISES

1. ὁ ἀδελφὸς τοῦ μαγείρου τὸν χοῖρον διώκει.

2. οἱ ἀδελφοὶ Κάδμου εἰσὶν ἔμποροι.

3. ὁ ἀδελφὸς Ἀλεξάνδρου οὔποτε ἔχει ἄργυρον ὅτι διδάσκαλός ἐστιν.

4. ὁ ἔμπορος διώκει τὸν ἀδελφὸν Τηλεμάχου.

5. διώκομεν τοὺς ἵππους τῶν γεωργῶν.

6. οἱ αἴλουροι Κάδμου ἐσθίουσιν τὸν τῡρὸν τῶν μαγείρων.

7. οἱ υἱοὶ τῶν γεωργῶν οὔποτε καθεύδουσιν.

8. ὑμεῖς οὐκ ἐστὲ ἰᾱτροί.

9. ἔχομεν χοίρους ὅτι γεωργοί ἐσμεν.

10. καθ᾽ ἡμέρᾱν ἐσθίει ἄρτον καὶ βούτῡρον ὁ υἱὸς τοῦ ἐμπόρου.

Answers on page 243.

LESSON 125

NEW WORD   διδάσκω

MEANING   *I teach*

You already know the noun διδάσκαλος which means *teacher*. Our new word for this lesson is based on the same root, but it's a verb instead of a noun.

The stem of this verb is διδασκ- so if you add the personal endings to the stem, you get the forms shown in the chart below.

	SINGULAR	PLURAL
FIRST PERSON	διδάσκω	διδάσκομεν
SECOND PERSON	διδάσκεις	διδάσκετε
THIRD PERSON	διδάσκει	διδάσκουσι(ν)

Here's an example sentence with our new verb for this lesson:

Κάδμος τοὺς γεωργοὺς διδάσκει. *(Cadmus is teaching the farmers.)*

EXERCISES

1. ὁ διδάσκαλος διδάσκει.

2. οἱ διδάσκαλοι διδάσκουσιν.

3. διδάσκω ὅτι διδάσκαλός εἰμι.

172

4. ὁ φιλόσοφος τοὺς υἱοὺς τοῦ Ἀλεξάνδρου διδάσκει.

5. ὁ διδάσκαλος διδάσκει Ἀλέξανδρον καὶ Κάδμον.

6. καθ' ἡμέρᾱν διδάσκομεν τοὺς υἱοὺς Τηλεμάχου.

7. Κάδμος πολλάκις διδάσκει ὅτι διδάσκαλός ἐστιν.

8. καθ' ἡμέρᾱν ὑμεῖς ἀγοράζετε τὸν βούτῡρον τῶν μαγείρων.

9. ὁ ἀδελφὸς Τηλεμάχου τοὺς αἰλούρους διώκει.

10. νῦν καθεύδω.

Answers on page 243.

LESSON 126

NEW WORD   θεῖος

MEANING   *uncle*

Over the past few lessons we have been learning the Greek words for certain family members such as *son* and *brother*. In this lesson, let's learn another one—the word for uncle.

Here is a chart showing the noun θεῖος along with the various noun endings that you have learned so far. Notice that the circumflex on the first syllable changes to an acute accent when the ending contains a long vowel or a diphthong that is considered long.

	SINGULAR	PLURAL
NOMINATIVE (SUBJ./PRED. NOM.)	ὁ θεῖος	οἱ θεῖοι
GENITIVE (POSSESSION)	τοῦ θείου	τῶν θείων
ACCUSATIVE (DIRECT OBJECT)	τὸν θεῖον	τοὺς θείους

And here is an example sentence using our new word:

ὁ θεῖος τοῦ Κάδμου ἐστὶ γεωργός. *(Cadmus's uncle is a farmer.)*

EXERCISES

1. οἱ θεῖοι Ἀλεξάνδρου εἰσὶν ἔμποροι.

174

2. ὁ θεῖος Τηλεμάχου ἔχει ἵππους καὶ χοίρους ὅτι γεωργός ἐστιν.

3. ὁ θεῖος τοῦ μαγείρου πάντοτε τῦρὸν ἔχει.

4. σὺ πολλάκις ἔχεις ἄργυρον καὶ χρῦσὸν ὅτι ἔμπορος εἶ.

5. Κάδμος διώκει τοὺς χοίρους τῶν γεωργῶν.

6. ἐγὼ οὔποτε διδάσκω ὅτι οὐκ εἰμὶ διδάσκαλος.

7. ὁ ἀδελφὸς Ἀλεξάνδρου βούτῡρον οὔποτε ἐσθίει.

8. οἱ ἵπποι τῶν γεωργῶν σπανίως καθεύδουσιν.

9. ὁ υἱὸς Κάδμου πολλάκις ἀναγιγνώσκει καὶ γράφει.

10. πολλάκις καθεύδουσιν οἱ αἴλουροι.

Answers on page 243.

LESSON 127

THE IOTA SUBSCRIPT

When the Greek alphabet was first developed, it did not have uppercase letters and lowercase letters. The only letters they had were the ones that we call uppercase. The lowercase letters were developed many hundreds of years later by medieval scribes. In medieval times, the printing press had not yet been invented, so these scribes spent many tedious hours copying books by hand. It was these scribes who developed the lowercase, cursive-looking Greek letters that are used today for ancient Greek texts (including this book). This kind of writing is called *minuscule.*

By the Medieval Period, the spelling and pronunciation of the Greek language had changed in certain ways, especially with vowels and diphthongs. Medieval scribes developed certain practices to indicate where spelling changes had taken place. In this lesson, I need to show you a certain writing practice that you should know something about. It involves the letter *iota.*

In ancient Greece, there were certain diphthongs called *long diphthongs.* These diphthongs consisted of a long vowel and the letter *iota.* When the ancient Greeks wrote a long diphthong, they would write the *iota* as a full-size letter, on the same line as all the other letters. Also, they pronounced the *iota* that was part of the long diphthong. But over time, ancient Greek speakers stopped pronouncing the *iota* in long diphthongs, so it became a silent letter. Instead of leaving out this silent *iota* altogether, Medieval scribes would write a small *iota* under the previous vowel. This small *iota* that sits under another vowel is called an *iota subscript.*

There are only three Greek vowels that can have an *iota* subscript. They are *alpha, eta,* and *omega.* Below, I have provided an example of each of these three vowels along with an *iota* subscript (in a large font size so you can get a good look at them).

Just for fun, let's compare the way that these long diphthongs would have been written in ancient Greece to the way they would be written today. Below I have provided a few examples taken from an ancient Greek inscription. I found this inscription by digging through an old antique book filled with inscriptions from ancient Greece. This particular inscription comes from ancient Athens, from around the year 398 BC, and it contains several words that I can use to show you how the *iota* subscript works. In the examples below, on the left you'll see the word as it originally appeared carved into stone, and then on the right you'll see how it appeared after the editor of the book converted it to regular Greek text.

176

I'll show one example of an *iota* subscript with an *alpha*, one with an *eta*, and one with an *omega*.

In this first example, there is a long *alpha* followed by an *iota*. On the left is the way this word looked as part of the ancient inscription, with the *iota* written as a full-size *iota* on the same line as the other letters. Then on the right is the way this exact same word would be written today in a printed Greek text, with the *iota* subscript parked under the letter *alpha*.

ΧΑΡΙΑΙ Χαρία

In this next example, the word ends with the letter *eta* followed by an *iota*. Again, on the left, the *iota* is written as a full-size *iota*, on the same line as the other letters. But today, that word would be written as shown on the right, with an *iota* subscript under the *eta*.

ΦΙΛΩΤΑΔΗΙ Φιλωτάδη

And finally, an example with the letter *omega*. On the left, the full-size *iota* is written on the same line as the other letters, but on the right it is an *iota* subscript parked under the *omega*.

ΕΥΒΙΩΙ Εὐβίῳ

The reason I'm telling you about the *iota* subscript is because you will soon encounter it in your own studies. In fact, the new noun ending that you will learn in the next lesson has an *iota* subscript.

When it comes to the pronunciation of the *iota* subscript, it's a long story—some Greek teachers pronounce it and others don't. In the pronunciation recordings that accompany this book, we will not pronounce the *iota* subscript, so just treat it as a silent letter.

LESSON 128

INDIRECT OBJECTS

The indirect object is the party in the sentence that is receiving or benefiting. In English indirect objects are often preceded by *to* or *for*. In each of the following examples, the indirect object is underlined. Notice how each is receiving or benefiting in the sentence.

> He gave the book to <u>Johnny</u>.
> She told a story to the <u>class</u>.
> She bought some presents for her <u>friends</u>.
> He showed his rock collection to <u>Mr. Green.</u>

And now, the same sentences but with a different word order:

> He gave <u>Johnny</u> the book.
> She told the <u>class</u> a story.
> She bought her <u>friends</u> some presents.
> He showed <u>Mr. Green</u> his rock collection.

So, although these two ways of expressing the indirect object are worded differently, they still mean the same thing.

By the way, take care not to confuse indirect objects with objects of a preposition. The *to* in an indirect object phrase tells us who is benefiting or receiving. When *to* is a preposition, it indicates physical motion or movement towards. Consider the following example:

> I sailed to the island.

In this example the word *to* is just a preposition, not an indication that what follows is an indirect object. Here's a good rule of thumb to remember: if you can replace *to* with *towards*, it is not an indirect object.

In the following exercises, see if you can identify the direct object and the indirect object.

EXERCISES

1. I loaned the money to my friend.
2. We donated money to the charity.
3. He showed the class an example.
4. Let's get some curtains for the house.
5. Henry got some seeds for the garden.
6. They made us some sandwiches.
7. He told the judge his story.
8. The band played another song for the audience.
9. I brought copies for everyone.
10. My mother bought me a shirt.

Answers on page 244.

LESSON 129

THE DATIVE CASE

The indirect object is the party in the sentence that is benefiting or receiving. In ancient Greek we indicate the indirect object in a sentence by using a case called the *dative case*. This case is shown on the third row of the chart below.

In the dative singular, the article is $\tau\hat{\omega}$ and the noun ending is $-\omega$. Look closely and you'll see that both this new article and new ending each have the letter *omega* along with an *iota* subscript tucked under it. The article $\tau\hat{\omega}$ will always have a circumflex. The noun ending $-\omega$ may or may not have an accent, depending on the word.

Observe the dative singular form in the chart below:

	SINGULAR	PLURAL
NOMINATIVE (SUBJ./PRED. NOM.)	ὁ γεωργός	οἱ γεωργοί
GENITIVE (POSSESSION)	τοῦ γεωργοῦ	τῶν γεωργῶν
DATIVE (INDIRECT OBJECT)	τῷ γεωργῷ	
ACCUSATIVE (DIRECT OBJECT)	τὸν γεωργόν	τοὺς γεωργούς

The dative case does not need the help of any other word to show the indirect object. In English, we can use words such as *to* and *for* to indicate the party that is benefiting or receiving. But in Greek these helper words are not necessary because the idea of *to* or *for* is embedded in the dative case itself.

Now that you know about indirect objects and the dative case, we can start to make Greek sentences that have an indirect object. Here's an example of the kind of sentence we can make:

I am giving the horse to the farmer.

In that sentence, the farmer is the indirect object—that is, he is the party that is receiving or benefiting. In a Greek sentence, we would use the dative case to show that the farmer is the indirect object. Let's do that now by putting the words *the* and *farmer* in the dative case.

I am giving the horse τῷ γεωργῷ.

So, if that were a complete Greek sentence, you would translate $\tau\hat{\omega}$ $\gamma\epsilon\omega\rho\gamma\hat{\omega}$ into English as *to the farmer* because it is the indirect object.

In the next lesson we will start to work with complete Greek sentences that contain an indirect object. But before we do that, take some time to study these examples. Notice that since the dative singular ending contains a long vowel, it can cause the accent in a noun to move or change.

- I am giving the gold $\tau\hat{\omega}$ $\dot{\epsilon}\mu\pi\acute{o}\rho\omega$ *(to the merchant)*.
- I am giving the pen $\tau\hat{\omega}$ $\delta\iota\delta\alpha\sigma\kappa\acute{a}\lambda\omega$ *(to the teacher)*.
- I am giving the bread $\dot{A}\lambda\epsilon\xi\acute{a}\nu\delta\rho\omega$ *(to Alexander)*.

LESSON 130

NEW WORD $\delta\acute{\iota}\delta\omega\mu\iota$

MEANING   *I give, I am giving*

PRONUNCIATION TIP: This word has the accent on the first syllable, so it sounds like *DEE-doh-me*.

In the last lesson you learned about the dative case and how it can be used to show who the indirect object is. We studied some very simple examples in which someone is giving something to someone. But if we want to be able to make that kind of sentence in Greek, you'll need to learn a new word—the Greek verb that means *give*. So that's our new word for this lesson.

The word $\delta\acute{\iota}\delta\omega\mu\iota$ is a first person singular verb that means *I give* or *I am giving*. It doesn't really look like any of the other action verbs you know, such as $\tau\rho\acute{\epsilon}\chi\omega$

181

or διδάσκω. That is because δίδωμι is part of a special class of verbs called -mi verbs. As you might guess, they are called -mi verbs because the first person singular form ends with -mi.

But actually, δίδωμι is not the first -mi verb you have learned. Think for a moment...do you know any other verbs that end with -mi? That's right— εἰμί is a -mi verb, too. But don't get too excited because εἰμί and δίδωμι don't really have the same characteristics. That's why in this lesson I'm only giving you the first person singular form of δίδωμι which is...um... δίδωμι.

Let's make a complete Greek sentence with δίδωμι, a direct object, and an indirect object:

δίδωμι τὸν ἵππον τῷ γεωργῷ. *(I am giving the horse to the farmer.)*

Of course, you can use ἐγώ with δίδωμι as with any other first person singular verb.

ἐγὼ δίδωμι τὸν κάλαμον τῷ φιλοσόφῳ. *(I am giving the pen to the philosopher.)*

Also, a noun in the dative case can be possessed by another noun in the genitive, like this:

ἄρτον δίδωμι τῷ υἱῷ τοῦ γεωργοῦ. *(I am giving bread to the farmer's son.)*

The word order with the indirect object can be flexible. In other words, the indirect object doesn't necessarily have to come after the direct object.

τῷ ἐμπόρῳ ἄργυρον δίδωμι. *(I am giving silver to the merchant.)*

So, don't depend on word order to figure out what each noun is doing. Instead, concentrate on the noun endings. The endings will tell you what role each noun is playing in the sentence.

1. δίδωμι τὸν τῡρὸν τῷ γεωργῷ.

2. δίδωμι χρῡσὸν καὶ ἄργυρον τῷ ἐμπόρῳ.

3. ἐγὼ σπανίως δίδωμι τῡρὸν τῷ μαγείρῳ.

4. Ἀλεξάνδρῳ τοὺς καλάμους οὐ δίδωμι.

5. οὐ δίδωμι ἄρτον τῷ υἱῷ Κάδμου.

6. σὺ καθ᾽ ἡμέρᾱν διδάσκεις ὅτι διδάσκαλος εἶ.

7. ὁ θεῖος τοῦ μαγείρου ἐστὶ γεωργός.

8. ἐγὼ τοὺς ἵππους τῶν γεωργῶν ἀγοράζω.

9. τῡρὸν καὶ βούτῡρον ὁ ἀδελφὸς τοῦ γεωργοῦ πάντοτε ἔχει.

10. οἱ υἱοὶ τοῦ ἰᾱτροῦ διώκουσι τὸν αἴλουρον.

Answers on page 244.

LESSON 131

NEW WORD   χόρτος

MEANING   *fodder*

Our new word for this lesson can mean *hay* or *grass*, meaning the kind of food that you would give to horses or cows. So in this book we will translate χόρτος as *fodder*, which is a general term for the kind of food you give farm animals.

Here are the various forms of χόρτος, including the dative singular form.

	SINGULAR	PLURAL
NOMINATIVE (SUBJ./PRED. NOM.)	ὁ χόρτος	οἱ χόρτοι
GENITIVE (POSSESSION)	τοῦ χόρτου	τῶν χόρτων
DATIVE (INDIRECT OBJECT)	τῷ χόρτῳ	
ACCUSATIVE (DIRECT OBJECT)	τὸν χόρτον	τοὺς χόρτους

Here's an example sentence with our new word for this lesson.

οἱ ἵπποι χόρτον ἔχουσιν.   *(The horses have fodder.)*

EXERCISES

1. δίδωμι χόρτον τῷ ἵππῳ.

2. οἱ ἵπποι χόρτον οὐκ ἔχουσιν.

184

3. καθ' ἡμέρᾱν δίδωμι χόρτον τῷ χοίρῳ ὅτι γεωργός εἰμι.

4. οἱ χοῖροι καὶ οἱ ἵπποι χόρτον ἔχουσιν.

5. ὁ αἴλουρος τὸν χόρτον τοῦ ἵππου ἐσθίει.

6. ἔχομεν χόρτον ὅτι ἵπποι ἐσμέν.

7. καθ' ἡμέρᾱν ἀγοράζω καλάμους ὅτι φιλόσοφός εἰμι.

8. ὁ αἴλουρος τοῦ φιλοσόφου τὸν τῡρὸν ἐσθίει.

9. Κάδμος τοὺς υἱοὺς τῶν ἐμπόρων πολλάκις διδάσκει.

10. ὁ ἀδελφὸς καὶ θεῖος Ἀλεξάνδρου εἰσὶν ἰᾱτροί.

Answers on page 244.

LESSON 132

THE DATIVE PLURAL

You already know that the indirect object is the party in the sentence that is receiving or benefiting. But what if the indirect object consists of more than one person or animal? In that case, the indirect object will be plural, and it will use the plural form of the dative case.

In the dative plural, the article is τοῖς and the noun ending is -οις. The article τοῖς will always have a circumflex accent. The noun ending -οις may or may not have an accent, depending on the word.

	SINGULAR	PLURAL
NOMINATIVE (SUBJ./PRED. NOM.)	ὁ γεωργός	οἱ γεωργοί
GENITIVE (POSSESSION)	τοῦ γεωργοῦ	τῶν γεωργῶν
DATIVE (INDIRECT OBJECT)	τῷ γεωργῷ	τοῖς γεωργοῖς
ACCUSATIVE (DIRECT OBJECT)	τὸν γεωργόν	τοὺς γεωργούς

Here are a few example sentences for you to study before you do the exercises.

- δίδωμι χρῡσὸν τοῖς διδασκάλοις. *(I am giving gold to the teachers.)*
- ἐγὼ βούτῡρον καὶ τῡρὸν δίδωμι τοῖς μαγείροις. *(I am giving butter and cheese to the cooks.)*
- πάντοτε δίδωμι χόρτον τοῖς ἵπποις καὶ τοῖς χοίροις. *(I always give fodder to the horses and pigs.)*

186

1. πολλάκις δίδωμι ἄρτον τοῖς υἱοῖς Κάδμου.

2. δίδωμι τοὺς χοίρους τοῖς γεωργοῖς.

3. δίδωμι καλάμους τοῖς φιλοσόφοις καὶ τοῖς διδασκάλοις.

4. καθ᾽ ἡμέρᾱν δίδωμι χόρτον τοῖς ἵπποις ὅτι γεωργός εἰμι.

5. ἄργυρον τῷ θείῳ Ἀλεξάνδρου οὔποτε δίδωμι.

6. ὁ Κάδμος πολλάκις ἄρτον καὶ βούτῡρον ἐσθίει.

7. ἡμεῖς οὔποτε διδάσκομεν ὅτι οὐκ ἐσμὲν διδάσκαλοι.

8. οἱ ἀδελφοὶ τοῦ ἰᾱτροῦ φιλόσοφοί εἰσιν.

9. ἔχω τοὺς καλάμους τῶν διδασκάλων.

10. ὁ χοῖρος ἐσθίει τὸν χόρτον τῶν ἵππων.

Answers on page 244.

LESSON 133

NEW WORD   ἀγρός

MEANING   *field*

Our new word for this lesson reminds me of the farmer who won an award for being out standing in his field. By the way, the word ἀγρός is related to English words such as *agriculture* and *agrarian*.

	SINGULAR	PLURAL
NOMINATIVE (SUBJ./PRED. NOM.)	ὁ ἀγρός	οἱ ἀγροί
GENITIVE (POSSESSION)	τοῦ ἀγροῦ	τῶν ἀγρῶν
DATIVE (INDIRECT OBJECT)	τῷ ἀγρῷ	τοῖς ἀγροῖς
ACCUSATIVE (DIRECT OBJECT)	τὸν ἀγρόν	τοὺς ἀγρούς

Here's an example sentence with our new word for this lesson:

ὁ γεωργὸς οὐκ ἔχει ἀγρόν.   *(The farmer does not have a field.)*

EXERCISES

1. δίδωμι τοὺς ἀγροὺς τῷ γεωργῷ.

2. δίδωμι Ἀλεξάνδρῳ τὸν ἀγρόν.

3. ἀγρὸν ἔχομεν ὅτι γεωργοί ἐσμεν.

4. δίδωμι τῡρὸν τοῖς υἱοῖς Κάδμου.

5. Τηλέμαχος καὶ Κάδμος οὐκ ἔχουσιν ἀγροὺς ὅτι οὐκ εἰσὶ γεωργοί.

6. ὁ ἔμπορος πάντοτε ἔχει χρῡσὸν καὶ ἄργυρον.

7. ἡμεῖς καθ᾽ ἡμέρᾱν τοὺς υἱοὺς τῶν ἰᾱτρῶν διδάσκομεν.

8. οἱ θεῖοι Κάδμου εἰσὶ στρατηγοί.

9. οἱ αἴλουροι τοῦ γεωργοῦ τὸν χόρτον οὐκ ἐσθίουσιν.

10. οἱ διδάσκαλοι ἄρτον καὶ βούτῡρον καθ᾽ ἡμέρᾱν ἐσθίουσιν.

Answers on page 244.

LESSON 134

NEW WORD   οἶκος

MEANING   *house*

PRONUNCIATION TIP: This word starts with the οι diphthong and a smooth breathing. The accent is on the first syllable, so it sounds something like *OY-kohs*.

Our new word for this lesson is related to the English word *economics*, which comes from Greek roots. The *eco-* part of the word, even though it doesn't look like it, is from the word οἶκος. The *-nom-* part the word is from the Greek word νόμος which means *law* or *custom*. These root words are seen combined in the ancient Greek word οἰκονομία which means *management of a household*. So that's why the word *economics* has to do with the management and movement of resources.

Here's a chart showing the various forms of οἶκος. Notice that when the noun ending contains a long vowel or a diphthong that is considered long, the circumflex accent will change to an acute accent.

	Singular	Plural
Nominative (SUBJ./PRED. NOM.)	ὁ οἶκος	οἱ οἶκοι
Genitive (POSSESSION)	τοῦ οἴκου	τῶν οἴκων
Dative (INDIRECT OBJECT)	τῷ οἴκῳ	τοῖς οἴκοις
Accusative (DIRECT OBJECT)	τὸν οἶκον	τοὺς οἴκους

190

Here's an example sentence with our new word for this lesson.

σπανίως ἀγοράζει ὁ ἔμπορος οἴκους. *(The merchant seldom buys houses.)*

EXERCISES

1. ὁ φιλόσοφος οὐκ ἔχει οἶκον.

2. οἱ γεωργοὶ ἔχουσιν ἀγροὺς καὶ οἴκους.

3. οὐκ ἔχετε οἶκον.

4. ἀγοράζομεν τὸν οἶκον Κάδμου.

5. οὐκ ἔχω οἶκον ὅτι φιλόσοφός εἰμι.

6. οἱ ἀδελφοὶ Κάδμου διδάσκαλοί εἰσιν.

7. ὁ μάγειρος πάντοτε ἀγοράζει τῡρὸν καὶ βούτῡρον.

8. ὁ χοῖρος διώκει τὸν αἴλουρον Ἀλεξάνδρου.

9. οὔποτε δίδωμι χόρτον τοῖς αἰλούροις.

10. οἱ φιλόσοφοι τοὺς υἱοὺς τῶν γεωργῶν σπανίως διδάσκουσιν.

Answers on page 245.

191

LESSON 135

THE VOCATIVE CASE

There is one last case to learn, but don't worry—it's easy. It's called the *vocative case.* The vocative case is what you use when you directly address someone. In each of these sentences, the underlined word is a noun in the vocative case.

- <u>Mom!</u> Give me my lunch money!
- <u>Officer!</u> I didn't realize I was speeding.
- <u>Fluffy!</u> Get off the kitchen table!

In each of these sentences, someone is addressing someone directly—Mom, a police officer, and Fluffy the cat. In ancient Greek, when we speak directly to someone or call out directly to someone in this manner, the person's name must be in the vocative case.

For all the nouns in this book, the vocative case will be formed in the same way. The vocative case is formed is by changing the ending from $-o\varsigma$ to $-\epsilon$ like this:

$$\text{Ἀλέξανδρος} \longrightarrow \text{Ἀλέξανδρε}$$

You will often see the interjection $\overset{\hat{}}{\omega}$ (pronounced *oh*) before a name in the vocative case, like this:

$$\overset{\hat{}}{\omega} \text{ Ἀλέξανδρε}$$

The interjection $\overset{\hat{}}{\omega}$ doesn't really translate to anything. It's similar to when we sometimes say *oh* in English, like this:

<u>Oh</u> Fred, I'm so sorry to hear about your pet llama.

Any time you directly address someone, you need to use the vocative case, as seen in these examples:

- $\overset{\hat{}}{\omega}$ γεωργέ *(Farmer!)*

- ὦ ἵππε *(Horse!)*
- ὦ Τηλέμαχε *(Telemachus!)*

If you want to call out to a group of people, you'll need to use the vocative plural. That is easy to do though, because the vocative plural is the same as the nominative plural. So if you want to call out to a group of farmers, you could say this:

ὦ γεωργοί *(Farmers!)*

As you can see, the interjection ὦ is the same whether the noun in the vocative is singular or plural. But even though ὦ is not an article, I will put it in the noun charts from now on just because it is so commonly associated with the vocative case.

	SINGULAR	PLURAL
NOMINATIVE (SUBJ./PRED. NOM.)	ὁ γεωργός	οἱ γεωργοί
GENITIVE (POSSESSION)	τοῦ γεωργοῦ	τῶν γεωργῶν
DATIVE (INDIRECT OBJECT)	τῷ γεωργῷ	τοῖς γεωργοῖς
ACCUSATIVE (DIRECT OBJECT)	τὸν γεωργόν	τοὺς γεωργούς
VOCATIVE (ADDRESS)	ὦ γεωργέ	ὦ γεωργοί

In this book, I will use ὦ with nouns in the vocative whenever possible to help you identify the vocative case more easily.

For a few Greek nouns, the accent will change for the vocative singular form of the noun. You'll see this especially with the words for members of the family, such as the Greek words for *father, husband, daughter,* and *brother.* You already know one of these words—the Greek word for *brother* which is ἀδελφός. Notice that for the word ἀδελφός, the accent is on the last syllable. But for the vocative singular form, the accent generally moves to the first syllable, becoming ἄδελφε. That is how the vocative singular of ἀδελφός will appear in this book.

Now let's take a look at some example sentences with the vocative case:

- ὦ Ἀλέξανδρε, οὐκ ἔχεις ἄρτον. *(Alexander, you do not have bread.)*

- ὦ αἴλουροι, ὑμεῖς πάντοτε καθεύδετε. *(Cats, y'all are always sleeping.)*

- ὦ ἄδελφε, σὺ οὐκ εἶ μάγειρος. *(Brother, you are not a cook.)*

EXERCISES

1. ὦ Ἀλέξανδρε, οὐκ εἶ μάγειρος.

2. ὦ ἵπποι, ἔχετε χόρτον.

3. ὦ αἴλουρε, σὺ πάντοτε καθεύδεις.

4. ὦ Κάδμε, σὺ οὐκ εἶ φιλόσοφος.

5. ὦ φιλόσοφοι, οὐκ ἔχετε οἴκους.

6. ὁ υἱὸς Κάδμου ἐστὶν ὁ θεῖος Τηλεμάχου.

7. σπανίως ἄρτον ἐσθίω.

8. Ἀλέξανδρος καὶ Τηλέμαχος τοὺς υἱοὺς τῶν ἐμπόρων διδάσκουσιν.

9. Κάδμος οὐκ ἔχει ἀγρὸν ὅτι γεωργὸς οὐκ ἔστιν.

10. δίδωμι χόρτον τοῖς ἵπποις.

Answers on page 245.

LESSON 136

REVIEW

Congratulations! You now have a basic familiarity with all five noun cases in ancient Greek. You've come a long way from lesson 1. Please take a moment to reflect on everything you have learned so far.

Here is a completed chart for the noun γεωργός.

	SINGULAR	PLURAL
NOMINATIVE (SUBJ./PRED. NOM.)	ὁ γεωργός	οἱ γεωργοί
GENITIVE (POSSESSION)	τοῦ γεωργοῦ	τῶν γεωργῶν
DATIVE (INDIRECT OBJECT)	τῷ γεωργῷ	τοῖς γεωργοῖς
ACCUSATIVE (DIRECT OBJECT)	τὸν γεωργόν	τοὺς γεωργούς
VOCATIVE (ADDRESS)	ὦ γεωργέ	ὦ γεωργοί

In Greek, noun endings are important because they indicate what role each noun is playing in a sentence, and how that particular noun will work together with the other words in the sentence. If we took only the noun endings and put them into a chart, here is what it would look like:

	SINGULAR	PLURAL
NOMINATIVE (SUBJ./PRED. NOM.)	-ος	-οι
GENITIVE (POSSESSION)	-ου	-ων
DATIVE (INDIRECT OBJECT)	-ῳ	-οις
ACCUSATIVE (DIRECT OBJECT)	-ον	-ους
VOCATIVE (ADDRESS)	-ε	-οι

All the nouns that you have learned so far in this book have that same pattern of endings. A pattern of endings such as this one is called a *declension* (pronounced *deh-KLEN-shun*). In ancient Greek there are three main declensions. We call these the first declension, the second declension, and the third declension.

Each of the three declensions has a different pattern of noun endings. The first declension is a pattern of endings that is used mostly by feminine nouns. The second declension is a pattern of endings used mainly by masculine nouns and neuter nouns. The third declension is a pattern of endings used by all three genders. In this book, I have limited the vocabulary only to masculine nouns of the second declension. This way, you can focus on only one pattern of endings, and you won't get confused by trying to learn two or three different patterns at the same time.

Since this book is limited only to masculine nouns of the second declension, you learned lots of masculine nouns such as the Greek words for *son, brother,* and *uncle.* Later in your Greek studies, you will learn the first declension. Then, you can learn feminine nouns such as the Greek word for *sister.* When you eventually learn the third declension, you can learn a variety of Greek nouns such as *father, mother, daughter,* and more. But for the moment, you are limited to only masculine nouns of the second declension.

The good news is that when you begin to study a new declension, you won't be starting from scratch. Since you already have a basic idea of how each case is used, you will just need to learn the new noun endings for that particular declension, and you'll be on your way. And that has been my strategy in this book—to give you a foundation of knowledge that you can build upon as you continue your Greek studies.

LESSON 137

MORE ABOUT δίδωμι

A few lessons ago (lesson 130) I introduced you to the word δίδωμι which means *I give* or *I am giving.* As I mentioned before, the reason that δίδωμι doesn't look like the other action verbs you know is because δίδωμι is part of a special class of verbs known as *-mi* verbs. These verbs are called *-mi* verbs, as you might guess, because the first person singular form ends in -μι.

Ever since you learned the word δίδωμι we have been able to make sentences in which someone is giving something to someone. This has allowed us to practice using the dative case in Greek to express indirect objects. But δίδωμι is only the first person singular form—you still don't know the other five present tense forms of this verb. So over the next few lessons, you will learn the other present tense forms of δίδωμι.

But before we start to learn more about *-mi* verbs, you should know that *-mi* verbs are not constructed in exactly the same way as the other action verbs you know. Earlier in this book you learned that each action verb has a stem and personal endings. You can take the stem of the verb, add a personal ending, and get whatever form of that verb you want. Let's say, for example, we want to make the second person singular form of the verb τρέχω. Here is how it would look:

$$τρεχ + εις = τρέχεις$$

But with *-mi* verbs, it's not that simple. With *-mi* verbs, the relationship between the stem and the personal endings is slightly more complicated—so for this reason, I won't say much about the stems and personal endings of *-mi* verbs, but I will give you a few observations that should make it easier for you to learn and remember these verbs. Also, we will take things slowly and learn only one verb form per lesson. Taking them one at a time will give you more of an opportunity to get accustomed to these new and unfamiliar verbs. So get ready to expand your knowledge of Greek verbs!

LESSON 138

NEW WORD   δίδως

MEANING   *you give, you are giving*

PRONUNCIATION TIP: The accent is on the first syllable, so this word sounds roughly like *DEE-dose*.

The second person singular form of δίδωμι is δίδως. Like other second person singular verbs, it ends with the letter *sigma*, but it doesn't have the same -εις ending as other second person singular verbs such as τρέχεις and ἔχεις.

	SINGULAR	PLURAL
FIRST PERSON	δίδωμι	
SECOND PERSON	(δίδως)	
THIRD PERSON		

Here's an example sentence with our new word for this lesson.

δίδως τὸν ἀγρὸν Ἀλεξάνδρῳ. *(You are giving the field to Alexander.)*

EXERCISES

1. οὔποτε δίδως χρῡσὸν τοῖς ἀδελφοῖς Τηλεμάχου.

2. σὺ δίδως ἄρτον τῷ υἱῷ τοῦ γεωργοῦ.

3. ὦ γεωργοί, πολλάκις δίδωμι ἄρτον τοῖς χοίροις.

4. ὦ στρατηγέ, ἵππον οὐκ ἔχεις.

5. καθ' ἡμέρᾱν ἀγοράζω βούτῡρον καὶ τῡρὸν τῶν ἐμπόρων.

6. ἔχουσιν οἱ γεωργοὶ ἀγροὺς καὶ οἴκους.

7. ἄρτον πολλάκις δίδωμι τοῖς υἱοῖς τοῦ διδασκάλου.

8. ὦ Κάδμε, σὺ οὐκ εἶ στρατηγός.

9. οἱ ἵπποι Ἀλεξάνδρου οὐκ ἔχουσιν χόρτον.

10. ἡμεῖς οὔποτε τρέχομεν ὅτι στρατηγοί ἐσμεν.

Answers on page 245.

LESSON 139

NEW WORD   δίδωσι(ν)

MEANING   *he/she/it gives, he/she/it is giving*

The third person singular form of δίδωμι has a movable *nu*. So if the next word starts with a consonant, it will be spelled δίδωσι. But if the next word starts with a vowel, or if this verb is the last word in the sentence, it will be spelled δίδωσιν.

This particular form of δίδωμι may confuse you a little at first because instead of a third person singular ending, it looks a lot like the third person plural ending that you are accustomed to. So try not to mix them up.

	SINGULAR	PLURAL
FIRST PERSON	δίδωμι	
SECOND PERSON	δίδως	
THIRD PERSON	δίδωσι(ν)	

Here's an example sentence with our new word for this lesson.

πολλάκις δίδωσι Τηλέμαχος ἄργυρον τοῖς ἐμπόροις. *(Telemachus often gives silver to the merchants.)*

EXERCISES

1. ὁ γεωργὸς τοῖς χοίροις χόρτον δίδωσιν.

2. ὁ φιλόσοφος δίδωσι τὸν κάλαμον τῷ διδασκάλῳ.

3. δίδως τὸν ἄρτον τῷ υἱῷ τοῦ μαγείρου.

4. δίδως τοῖς γεωργοῖς τὸν ἀγρὸν ὅτι οὐκ ἔχουσιν ἀγρούς.

5. ὁ θεῖος Κάδμου οὔποτε χρῦσὸν ἔχει.

6. ὁ ἔμπορος δίδωσιν ἄρτον τοῖς φιλοσόφοις.

7. ὁ ἰᾱτρὸς αἰλούρους ἔχει.

8. καθεύδω νῦν ὅτι αἴλουρός εἰμι.

9. ὦ φιλόσοφε, οἶκον οὐκ ἔχεις.

10. οἱ γεωργοὶ τοὺς ἵππους διώκουσιν.

Answers on page 245.

LESSON 140

NEW WORD   δίδομεν

MEANING   *we give, we are giving*

The first person plural form of δίδωμι shouldn't be too hard to remember because its ending is similar to the other first person plural verbs you know such as τρέχομεν and γράφομεν.

Notice that the singular forms of δίδωμι have an *omega*, but our new form for this lesson has an *omicron* instead. More about this later.

	SINGULAR	PLURAL
FIRST PERSON	δίδωμι	δίδομεν
SECOND PERSON	δίδως	
THIRD PERSON	δίδωσι(ν)	

Here's an example sentence with our new word for this lesson.

δίδομεν χόρτον τοῖς ἵπποις.   *(We are giving fodder to the horses.)*

EXERCISES

1. οὔποτε δίδομεν βούτῡρον τοῖς ἐμπόροις.

2. πολλάκις ἄρτον δίδομεν τοῖς υἱοῖς Τηλεμάχου.

3. ὁ ἀδελφὸς Κάδμου δίδωσι τῷ γεωργῷ τοὺς χοίρους.

4. ὦ υἱέ, σὺ οὐκ εἶ στρατηγός.

5. Ἀλέξανδρος καθ' ἡμέρᾱν διώκει τοὺς ἵππους τῶν γεωργῶν.

6. Κάδμος καὶ Τηλέμαχος οὐκ ἔχουσιν οἶκον ὅτι φιλόσοφοί εἰσιν.

7. ὦ ἄδελφε, σὺ μάγειρος οὐκ εἶ.

8. ὁ γεωργὸς δίδωσι τοὺς ἀγροὺς Ἀλεξάνδρῳ.

9. ὁ θεῖος Κάδμου πάντοτε καθεύδει.

10. οἱ αἴλουροι πάντοτε καθεύδουσιν.

Answers on page 245.

LESSON 141

NEW WORD   δίδοτε

MEANING   *y'all give, y'all are giving*

Here's another form of δίδωμι that shouldn't be hard to remember. This verb ends with -τε like the other second person plural verbs you know such as ἀναγιγνώσκετε and ἔχετε.

And again, notice that there is an *omicron* where the singular forms have an *omega*.

	SINGULAR	PLURAL
FIRST PERSON	δίδωμι	δίδομεν
SECOND PERSON	δίδως	δίδοτε
THIRD PERSON	δίδωσι(ν)	

Here's an example sentence with our new word for this lesson.

ὑμεῖς τῷ Κάδμῳ ἄρτον καὶ βούτῡρον δίδοτε. *(Y'all are giving bread and butter to Cadmus.)*

EXERCISES

1. πολλάκις δίδοτε χόρτον τοῖς ἵπποις ὅτι ἐστὲ γεωργοί.

2. οὔποτε δίδοτε χρῡσὸν τῷ θείῳ Κάδμου.

204

3. καθ' ἡμέρᾱν δίδομεν ἄρτον καὶ βούτῡρον τοῖς φιλοσόφοις ὅτι ἄρτον οὐκ ἔχουσιν.

4. ὁ στρατηγὸς δίδωσι τὸν οἶκον Ἀλεξάνδρῳ.

5. δίδως ἄργυρον τοῖς υἱοῖς τῶν ἐμπόρων.

6. οἱ φιλόσοφοι διδάσκουσι τοὺς ἀδελφοὺς Τηλεμάχου.

7. ὁ ἔμπορος τὸν ἀγρὸν ἀγοράζει.

8. ἔχομεν χοίρους καὶ ἵππους ὅτι γεωργοί ἐσμεν.

9. σπανίως τῡρὸν ἐσθίω.

10. ὦ Κάδμε, σὺ οὐκ εἶ στρατηγός.

Answers on page 246.

LESSON 142

NEW WORD   διδόασι(ν)

MEANING   *they give, they are giving*

PRONUNCIATION TIP: In this form of δίδωμι, notice that there is both an *omicron* and an *alpha* next to each other. These two vowels do not form a diphthong, so each vowel gets its own syllable. Also, it has a movable *nu* at the end, so it will sound like *dee-DOH-aah-see* or *dee-DOH-aah-seen*.

Our chart is now full!

	SINGULAR	PLURAL
FIRST PERSON	δίδωμι	δίδομεν
SECOND PERSON	δίδως	δίδοτε
THIRD PERSON	δίδωσι(ν)	διδόασι(ν)

Here's an example sentence with our new word for this lesson.

οἱ διδάσκαλοι καλάμους τοῖς φιλοσόφοις διδόασιν.
(The teachers are giving pens to the philosophers.)

EXERCISES

1. οἱ υἱοὶ τοῦ γεωργοῦ διδόασι τῡρὸν καὶ βούτῡρον τοῖς μαγείροις.

2. ὁ στρατηγὸς τῷ ἐμπόρῳ χρῡσὸν δίδωσιν.

206

3. δίδοτε καλάμους Ἀλεξάνδρῳ.

4. ἡμεῖς χόρτον οὔποτε δίδομεν τοῖς ἵπποις ὅτι οὐκ ἐσμὲν γεωργοί.

5. ὁ ἀδελφὸς Κάδμου δίδωσι τοὺς ἀγροὺς τοῖς γεωργοῖς.

6. σὺ δίδως τοὺς καλάμους τοῖς φιλοσόφοις.

7. οἱ θεῖοι Ἀλεξάνδρου οὐκ εἰσὶν ἰατροί.

8. οὔποτε ἀναγιγνώσκουσιν οἱ ἵπποι.

9. τὸν υἱὸν τοῦ ἐμπόρου καθ' ἡμέρᾱν διδάσκω ὅτι διδάσκαλός εἰμι.

10. ὁ αἴλουρος τοῦ γεωργοῦ τοὺς χοίρους διώκει.

Answers on page 246.

LESSON 143

REVIEW OF δίδωμι

Now that you know all six present tense forms of δίδωμι, let's take a moment to examine these verb forms as a group. And as we do, we can review a couple of the observations I pointed out earlier.

Here is the verb chart again:

	SINGULAR	PLURAL
FIRST PERSON	δίδωμι	δίδομεν
SECOND PERSON	δίδως	δίδοτε
THIRD PERSON	δίδωσι(ν)	διδόασι(ν)

Now that all six forms are here in one place, it will be a bit easier for you to compare them. Notice again that in the singular forms of this verb, the vowel before the personal ending is an *omega*: δίδωμι, δίδως, and δίδωσι(ν). But in the plural forms, the vowel that comes before the personal ending is an *omicron*: δίδομεν, δίδοτε, and διδόασι(ν). Remember that *omega* and *omicron* are the same except that *omega* is long and *omicron* is short. So here is something to remember about *-mi* verbs: the singular forms of a *-mi* verb will have a long vowel, but the plural forms will have a short vowel.

Another helpful observation is that the third person plural has one syllable more than the other present tense forms. Notice that the accent is on the *omicron*, but then after that there is an *alpha* which makes a separate syllable. So διδόασιν would sound like *dee-DOH-ah-seen*.

The ending of the third person singular form δίδωσι(ν) looks similar to the third person plural verbs you know, so try to remember that it is singular, not plural.

And lastly, notice again that both the third person singular and third person plural forms of δίδωμι have a movable *nu*. The other *-mi* verb you know, εἰμί, also has this same characteristic—think of ἐστί(ν) and εἰσί(ν). This is different from the other action verbs you know which only have a movable *nu* in the third person plural, but *not* in the third person singular.

LESSON 144

PREPOSITIONS

A *preposition* is a word that shows a relationship or connection between two nouns. Examples of prepositions are *in, to, from, below, above,* and *beside.* Here's an example of a sentence with a preposition.

The bicycle is inside the garage.

In that sentence, the word *inside* is a preposition. Notice that in this sentence there are two items being talked about: the bicycle and the garage. The preposition showed the relationship between the two items.

The person saying this sentence wants to tell someone about the location of the bicycle. There are several ways to tell someone the location of an item. The speaker could have indicated the location of the bicycle a different way. If the bicycle happened to be nearby, the speaker could have simply pointed at it and said, "It's over here," or "It's over there." But with a preposition, you don't have to be near the object you want to talk about—you can use words to indicate its location by using something else as a point of reference. Prepositions can show

209

relationships in space, time, or even in abstract concepts such as thoughts or ideas.

Let's look at that sentence again and observe how the speaker used the garage as a way to specify the location of the bicycle.

The bicycle is inside the garage.

The speaker used the garage as a point of reference to show where the bicycle was. The preposition *inside* referred directly to the garage. In grammatical terms, the word that the preposition refers to is called the *object of the preposition.* Therefore, in this sentence, the word *inside* is the preposition and the word *garage* is the object of the preposition.

Just for practice, in each of the following sentences, see if you can spot the preposition and the object of the preposition.

EXERCISES

1. Your book fell behind the couch.
2. Just put that plant beside the lamp.
3. The spare tire is in the trunk.
4. We drove through the tunnel.
5. I just saw a chipmunk run under the house!
6. I want to get this done before lunch.
7. After school, the accordion ensemble will rehearse again.
8. The new store is by the post office.
9. You aren't allowed to do that on campus.
10. Have you ever wondered what is beyond that mountain?

Answers on page 246.

LESSON 145

PREPOSITIONS IN ANCIENT GREEK

In ancient Greek, each preposition works with certain noun cases. Whenever there is a preposition in a Greek sentence, the object of the preposition cannot be in the nominative case. Instead, it must be in one of the following three cases:

- genitive
- dative
- accusative

According to the rules of Greek grammar, some prepositions can work with only one particular case—but other prepositions can work with two or even all three of these cases! In this book I will keep the usage of prepositions extremely simple so you can get some basic experience working with them. Also, I'll give you some general rules that will help you understand how Greek prepositions work.

LESSON 146

PREPOSITIONS WITH THE GENITIVE CASE

Back in lesson 121 you learned that the genitive case can be used to show possession. But, as I mentioned in the last lesson, the genitive case can also be used as the object of a preposition.

Greek prepositions that indicate movement away from something generally take the genitive case. For example, the genitive case could be used to express that something is moving away from a house or out of a house, as seen in these prepositional phrases:

- from the house
- out of the house

To make prepositional phrases like those in ancient Greek, you would put the word for *house* in the genitive case. To demonstrate this, we will mix English and Greek while a helpful cat demonstrates the action.

- from *τοῦ οἴκου*

- out of *τοῦ οἴκου*

Now you know two different ways that the genitive case can be used: 1) to show possession and 2) as the object of a preposition. You're making progress!

LESSON 147

PREPOSITIONS WITH THE DATIVE CASE

Way back in lesson 129 you learned that in Greek, the dative case is used to indicate the indirect object in a sentence. But, just like the genitive case, the dative case can also be used as the object of a preposition.

Greek prepositions that show that something is staying in one place generally take the dative case. For example, the dative case could be used to express that something is inside something, on top of something, or beside something, as seen in these prepositional phrases:

- in the house
- on the house
- beside the house

To make that kind of prepositional phrase in Greek, you would put the word for *house* in the dative case. Again, a hardworking cat will demonstrate the action as we mix English and Greek.

- in τῷ οἴκῳ

- on τῷ οἴκῳ

- beside τῷ οἴκῳ

Now you know two ways that the dative case can be used: 1) to show the indirect object and 2) as the object of a preposition. Nice work!

LESSON 148

PREPOSITIONS WITH THE ACCUSATIVE CASE

Way back in lesson 103, even though you didn't know the word "accusative" yet, you were learning about how the accusative case is used to indicate the direct object in a sentence. But, just like the genitive and dative cases, the accusative case can also be used as the object of a preposition.

In ancient Greek, prepositions that show that something is moving toward something generally take the accusative case. For example, the accusative case could be used to express that something is moving toward or into a house, as seen in these prepositional phrases:

- to the house
- into the house

To make that kind of prepositional phrase in Greek, you would put the word for *house* in the accusative case, like this (a well-behaved cat will again demonstrate the action):

- to τὸν οἶκον

- into τὸν οἶκον

Now you know two different ways to use the accusative case: 1) as a direct object and 2) as the object of a preposition. You are growing in your knowledge of Greek grammar!

Over the past few lessons you have learned that Greek prepositions can work with the genitive, dative, or accusative cases. Prepositions that show movement away from something generally take the genitive case. Prepositions that show that something is remaining still generally take the dative case. Prepositions that show movement toward something generally take the accusative case. These broad generalizations will not explain every use of every preposition, but they will give you a good way to visualize Greek prepositions and organize them in your mind. And just in time too, because in the next lesson you will begin working with your first real Greek preposition.

<hr>

LESSON 149

NEW WORD   ἐν

MEANING   *in*

PRONUNCIATION TIP: Notice that this particular preposition does not have an accent. Instead, it joins its syllable to the word that follows. This kind of word is called a *proclitic* (the opposite of an enclitic).

In the last lesson you learned that ancient Greek prepositions work with the genitive, dative, or accusative cases. Generally speaking, prepositions that show movement away from something use the genitive case. Prepositions that show that something is staying in one place take the dative case. Prepositions that show movement toward something use the accusative case.

In this lesson you are learning your first real Greek preposition, the word ἐν which means *in*. Since ἐν shows that something is staying in one place and not moving anywhere, it takes the dative case.

Here's an example sentence—our dependable cat is back to help demonstrate.

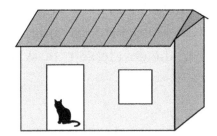

ὁ αἴλουρός ἐστιν ἐν τῷ οἴκῳ.
(The cat is in the house.)

In that sentence the word *house* was the object of the preposition ἐν, so both the definite article and the noun were in the dative case, giving us τῷ οἴκῳ.

Note that the object of a preposition can be plural as seen in this example:

οἱ ἵπποι ἐν τοῖς ἀγροῖς εἰσιν. *(The horses are in the fields.)*

In the following exercises, watch out for prepositional phrases with the preposition ἐν plus the dative case.

EXERCISES

1. ὁ χοῖρος ἐν τῷ οἴκῳ ἐστίν.

2. ὁ ἵππος ἐστὶν ἐν τῷ ἀγρῷ.

3. ὁ γεωργὸς οὐκ ἔστιν ἐν τῷ οἴκῳ.

4. οἱ αἴλουροί εἰσιν ἐν τῷ οἴκῳ.

5. ὁ ἔμπορος δίδωσι τὸν χοῖρον τῷ γεωργῷ.

6. οἱ αἴλουροι καθεύδουσιν ἐν τῷ οἴκῳ.

7. οὔποτε τρέχω ἐν τῷ οἴκῳ.

8. Κάδμος τῷ διδασκάλῳ τὸν κάλαμον δίδωσιν.

9. ὦ ἵππε, σὺ οὐκ εἶ χοῖρος.

10. δίδομεν ἄρτον Ἀλεξάνδρῳ ὅτι ἄρτον οὐκ ἔχει.

Answers on page 246.

LESSON 150

NEW WORD   ποταμός

MEANING   *river*

Way back in lesson 88 I told you that the English word *hippopotamus* was made up of the Greek words for *horse* and *river*. The word ἵππος makes up the first part of the word, while our new word for this lesson makes up the second part: the word ποταμός which means *river*.

	SINGULAR	PLURAL
NOMINATIVE (SUBJ./PRED. NOM.)	ὁ ποταμός	οἱ ποταμοί
GENITIVE (POSSESSION)	τοῦ ποταμοῦ	τῶν ποταμῶν
DATIVE (INDIRECT OBJECT)	τῷ ποταμῷ	τοῖς ποταμοῖς
ACCUSATIVE (DIRECT OBJECT)	τὸν ποταμόν	τοὺς ποταμούς
VOCATIVE (ADDRESS)	ὦ ποταμέ	ὦ ποταμοί

Here's an example sentence using the new word for our "current" lesson.

ὁ ἵππος ἐστὶν ἐν τῷ ποταμῷ. *(The horse is in the river.)*

EXERCISES

1. ὁ χοῖρος Κάδμου ἐν τῷ ποταμῷ ἐστιν.

2. οἱ υἱοὶ τῶν γεωργῶν ἐν τῷ ποταμῷ εἰσιν.

3. οἱ ἵπποι εἰσὶν ἐν τοῖς ποταμοῖς.

4. ὁ υἱὸς Κάδμου ἐστὶν ἐν τῷ οἴκῳ.

5. Κάδμος καὶ Ἀλέξανδρός εἰσιν ἐν τῷ ποταμῷ.

6. δίδως τὸν χρῡσὸν τοῖς ἐμπόροις.

7. οἱ φιλόσοφοι ἐν τῷ οἴκῳ ἀναγιγνώσκουσιν.

8. ὁ θεῖος Τηλεμάχου ἐστὶ στρατηγός.

9. οἱ χοῖροί εἰσιν ἐν τοῖς ἀγροῖς.

10. πάντοτε χόρτον τῷ ἵππῳ δίδομεν.

Answers on page 246.

LESSON 151

NEW WORD   πρός

MEANING   *to, toward*

Prepositions that show something is moving toward something else generally take the accusative case. And since the preposition πρός means *to* or *toward*, it takes the accusative case. Try to use the translation that sounds the most natural in each situation.

Here's an example sentence, along with a helpful cat to demonstrate.

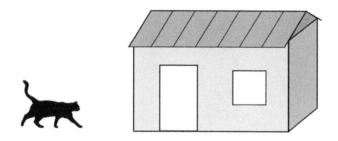

ὁ αἴλουρος τρέχει πρὸς τὸν οἶκον.
(The cat is running to the house.)

In that sentence the word *house* was the object of the preposition πρός, so both the definite article and the noun were in the accusative case, giving us τὸν οἶκον.

EXERCISES

1. Κάδμος πρὸς τὸν οἶκον τρέχει.

2. οἱ υἱοὶ τῶν γεωργῶν τρέχουσι πρὸς τοὺς ἀγρούς.

3. Τηλέμαχος καὶ Ἀλέξανδρος τρέχουσιν πρὸς τὸν ποταμόν.

4. οἱ ἵπποι τρέχουσιν πρὸς τὸν γεωργὸν ὅτι χόρτον ἔχει.

5. ὁ υἱὸς τοῦ γεωργοῦ ἐστιν ἐν τῷ ποταμῷ.

6. ὁ χόρτος ἐν τῷ ἀγρῷ ἐστιν.

7. Κάδμος διώκει τὸν χοῖρον πρὸς τοὺς οἴκους.

8. ὦ αἴλουρε, σὺ πάντοτε καθεύδεις.

9. οἱ γεωργοὶ νῦν διδόασι χόρτον τοῖς χοίροις.

10. οἱ διδάσκαλοι ἐν τῷ οἴκῳ διδάσκουσιν.

Answers on page 247.

LESSON 152

NEW WORD   βαδίζω

MEANING   *I walk, I am walking*

PRONUNCIATION TIP: The letter *zeta* sounds like a combination of the letter *z* and the letter *d*, like the *sd* in the word *wisdom*. So βαδίζω sounds like *ba-DEEZ-doe.*

For about the last 20 lessons you have been learning the various forms of the verb δίδωμι which is a -μι verb. But our new verb for this lesson is not a -μι verb—it's just a normal action verb like ἔχω, τρέχω, and διώκω.

So far, you only know one verb that can show that someone is going somewhere—the verb τρέχω. But now that we are working with prepositions, we need more verbs that can get people moving around. So in this lesson I'll teach you the verb βαδίζω, which means *walk*.

The stem of this verb is βαδιζ- so if you add the personal endings you'll get the forms in the chart below.

	SINGULAR	PLURAL
FIRST PERSON	βαδίζω	βαδίζομεν
SECOND PERSON	βαδίζεις	βαδίζετε
THIRD PERSON	βαδίζει	βαδίζουσι(ν)

221

Here's an example sentence using our new word for this lesson.

βαδίζομεν πρὸς τὸν οἶκον τοῦ Κάδμου. *(We are walking to Cadmus's house.)*

EXERCISES

1. καθ᾽ ἡμέρᾱν βαδίζω πρὸς τὸν ποταμόν.

2. ὁ γεωργὸς πρὸς τὸν ἀγρὸν βαδίζει.

3. οἱ υἱοὶ Ἀλεξάνδρου πρὸς τοὺς οἴκους βαδίζουσιν.

4. οὔποτε βαδίζομεν πρὸς τοὺς ἀγροὺς ὅτι ἡμεῖς οὐκ ἐσμὲν γεωργοί.

5. ὁ θεῖος Κάδμου καθεύδει ἐν τῷ οἴκῳ.

6. ὁ γεωργὸς τοὺς χοίρους πρὸς τὸν ἀγρὸν διώκει.

7. τρέχουσιν οἱ ἵπποι πρὸς τοὺς ἀγρούς.

8. οἱ χοῖροί εἰσιν ἐν τοῖς οἴκοις.

9. ἐγὼ οὔποτε ἀγοράζω τὸν βούτῡρον τοῦ γεωργοῦ.

10. ὦ στρατηγέ, οὐκ ἔχομεν ἵππους.

Answers on page 247.

LESSON 153

NEW WORD   ἀπό

MEANING   *from*

PRONUNCIATION TIP: Our new word for this lesson is similar to the word οὐ/οὐκ/οὐχ. If the next word begins with a consonant, it will be spelled ἀπό. If the next word begins with a vowel with a smooth breathing, it will be spelled ἀπ᾽. And if the next word begins with a vowel with a rough breathing, it will be spelled ἀφ᾽.

Prepositions that show something is moving away from something else generally take the genitive case. And since the preposition ἀπό means *from*, it takes the genitive case.

Here's an example sentence, along with a dependable cat to demonstrate.

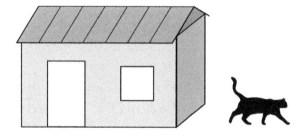

ὁ αἴλουρος τρέχει ἀπὸ τοῦ οἴκου.
(The cat is running from house.)

EXERCISES

1. βαδίζω ἀπὸ τοῦ οἴκου πρὸς τὸν ποταμόν.

2. βαδίζομεν ἀπὸ τοῦ ποταμοῦ πρὸς τὸν ἀγρόν.

223

3. Ἀλέξανδρος ἀπὸ τῶν ἀγρῶν βαδίζει πρὸς τὸν οἶκον.

4. οἱ γεωργοὶ ἐν τοῖς ἀγροῖς εἰσιν.

5. ὁ στρατηγὸς δίδωσιν ἵππον Κάδμῳ.

6. καθεύδουσιν οἱ αἴλουροι ἐν τῷ οἴκῳ.

7. οἱ ἵπποι πρὸς τὸν ποταμὸν τρέχουσιν.

8. ὦ Τηλέμαχε, σὺ οὐκ ἔχεις ἵππον.

9. ὁ υἱὸς τοῦ γεωργοῦ πρὸς τὸν ποταμὸν τρέχει.

10. ὦ αἴλουρε, σὺ οὐκ ἔχεις χόρτον.

Answers on page 247.

LESSON 154

NEW WORD   δρῡμός

MEANING   *woods*

PRONUNCIATION TIP: The *upsilon* in this word has a macron, indicating that it is long (don't forget to round your lips). This word sounds something like *droo-MOHS.*

The word δρῡμός means *a group of trees* or *woods.* In this book, for the sake of simplicity, let's translate it as *woods.*

	SINGULAR	PLURAL
NOMINATIVE (SUBJ./PRED. NOM.)	ὁ δρῡμός	οἱ δρῡμοί
GENITIVE (POSSESSION)	τοῦ δρῡμοῦ	τῶν δρῡμῶν
DATIVE (INDIRECT OBJECT)	τῷ δρῡμῷ	τοῖς δρῡμοῖς
ACCUSATIVE (DIRECT OBJECT)	τὸν δρῡμόν	τοὺς δρῡμούς
VOCATIVE (ADDRESS)	ὦ δρῡμέ	ὦ δρῡμοί

Here's an example sentence using our new word for this lesson.

ὁ ἵππος πρὸς τὸν δρῡμὸν τρέχει. *(The horse is running toward the woods.)*

EXERCISES

1. Τηλέμαχος πρὸς τὸν δρῡμὸν βαδίζει.

2. ὁ ἵππος ἐστὶν ἐν τῷ δρῡμῷ.

3. οἱ υἱοὶ τοῦ γεωργοῦ βαδίζουσι πρὸς τὸν δρῡμόν.

4. βαδίζομεν ἀπὸ τοῦ δρῡμοῦ πρὸς τὸν ποταμόν.

5. οἱ χοῖροι ἀπὸ τοῦ ἀγροῦ πρὸς τὸν δρῡμόν τρέχουσιν.

6. οἱ αἴλουροι πρὸς τοὺς οἴκους τρέχουσιν.

7. ὁ θεῖος Κάδμου ἐν τῷ δρῡμῷ καθεύδει.

8. ὦ χοῖρε, σὺ οὐκ εἶ ἵππος.

9. ὁ ἰᾱτρὸς τοῖς υἱοῖς Ἀλεξάνδρου ἄρτον δίδωσιν.

10. οἱ αἴλουροι ἀπὸ τῶν χοίρων τρέχουσιν.

Answers on page 247.

LESSON 155

NEW WORD   εἰς

MEANING   *into*

PRONUNCIATION TIP: Like ἐν, εἰς is a proclitic, so it doesn't have an accent.

Prepositions that show motion toward something generally take the accusative case. And, since the preposition εἰς means *into*, it takes the accusative case.

Here's an example sentence, along with a reliable cat to demonstrate.

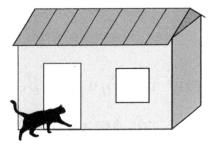

ὁ αἴλουρος τρέχει εἰς τὸν οἶκον.
(The cat is running into the house.)

EXERCISES

1. οἱ χοῖροι εἰς τὸν δρῡμὸν τρέχουσιν.

2. ὁ υἱὸς Ἀλεξάνδρου βαδίζει εἰς τὸν οἶκον.

3. ὦ Κάδμε, εἰς τὸν δρῡμὸν βαδίζομεν.

4. οἱ ἵπποι τρέχουσιν εἰς τοὺς ἀγρούς.

5. οἱ υἱοὶ τῶν γεωργῶν εἰς τὸν οἶκον τρέχουσιν.

6. ὁ στρατηγός ἐστιν ἐν τῷ δρῡμῷ.

226

7. ὁ διδάσκαλος δίδωσι τοὺς καλάμους τοῖς φιλοσόφοις.

8. οὐ βαδίζομεν πρὸς τὸν ποταμόν.

9. ὁ χοῖρος τρέχει ἀπὸ τοῦ μαγείρου.

10. Κάδμος καὶ Ἀλέξανδρος βαδίζουσιν ἀπὸ τοῦ δρῡμοῦ πρὸς τὸν ποταμόν.

Answers on page 247.

LESSON 156

NEW WORD   αἰγιαλός

MEANING   *beach*

Our new word for this lesson is "shore" to get your attention. Here is a chart with the various forms of αἰγιαλός.

	SINGULAR	PLURAL
NOMINATIVE (SUBJ./PRED. NOM.)	ὁ αἰγιαλός	οἱ αἰγιαλοί
GENITIVE (POSSESSION)	τοῦ αἰγιαλοῦ	τῶν αἰγιαλῶν
DATIVE (INDIRECT OBJECT)	τῷ αἰγιαλῷ	τοῖς αἰγιαλοῖς
ACCUSATIVE (DIRECT OBJECT)	τὸν αἰγιαλόν	τοὺς αἰγιαλούς
VOCATIVE (ADDRESS)	ὦ αἰγιαλέ	ὦ αἰγιαλοί

227

And here's an example sentence:

οἱ ἔμποροι πρὸς τὸν αἰγιαλὸν βαδίζουσιν. *(The merchants are walking to the beach.)*

EXERCISES

1. Ἀλέξανδρος βαδίζει ἀπὸ τοῦ οἴκου πρὸς τὸν αἰγιαλόν.

2. οἱ ἵπποι τρέχουσι πρὸς τὸν αἰγιαλόν.

3. οἱ αδελφοὶ Κάδμου ἀπὸ τοῦ αἰγιαλοῦ βαδίζουσιν πρὸς τὸν δρῡμόν.

4. οὔποτε βαδίζω πρὸς τὸν αἰγιαλόν.

5. βαδίζομεν εἰς τὸν δρῡμόν.

6. ὁ χοῖρος καθεύδει ἐν τῷ οἴκῳ.

7. οἱ ἔμποροι ἀπὸ τοῦ αἰγιαλοῦ πρὸς τὸν ποταμὸν βαδίζουσιν.

8. ἐγὼ πολλάκις ἄρτον Ἀλεξάνδρῳ δίδωμι.

9. ὁ χρῡσός ἐστιν ἐν τῷ δρῡμῷ.

10. ὁ υἱὸς τοῦ γεωργοῦ ἀπὸ τῶν χοίρων τρέχει.

Answers on page 248.

LESSON 157

NEW WORD ἐκ/ἐξ

MEANING   *out of*

PRONUNCIATION TIP: Like ἐν and εἰς, ἐκ/ἐξ is a proclitic, so it doesn't have an accent.

Our new word for this lesson has two different spellings. If the next word starts with a consonant, it will be spelled ἐκ. If the next word starts with a vowel, it will be spelled ἐξ.

Prepositions that show motion away from something usually take the genitive case. And since ἐκ/ἐξ means *out of*, it takes the genitive case.

Here's an example sentence, along with a well-behaved cat to demonstrate.

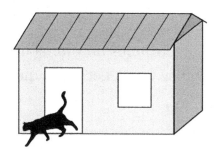

ὁ αἴλουρος τρέχει ἐκ τοῦ οἴκου.
(The cat is running out of the house.)

EXERCISES

1. οἱ ἵπποι τρέχουσιν ἐκ τοῦ δρῡμοῦ.

2. ὁ γεωργὸς ἐκ τοῦ οἴκου βαδίζει πρὸς τοὺς ἀγρούς.

3. Τηλέμαχος διώκει τὸν αἴλουρον ἐκ τοῦ οἴκου.

4. οὔποτε καθεύδω ἐν τῷ δρῡμῷ.

5. καθ᾽ ἡμέρᾱν οἱ ἔμποροι πρὸς τὸν αἰγιαλὸν βαδίζουσιν.

229

6. Ἀλέξανδρος ἀπὸ τοῦ ποταμοῦ πρὸς τὸν οἶκον βαδίζει.

7. δίδομεν χόρτον τοῖς ἵπποις ὅτι γεωργοί ἐσμεν.

8. οὔποτε βαδίζεις πρὸς τὸν αἰγιαλόν.

9. ὁ χοῖρος εἰς τὸν δρῡμὸν τρέχει.

10. ἐγώ εἰμι γεωργός.

Answers on page 248.

LESSON 158

REVIEW OF PREPOSITIONS

You have been working with prepositions now for about the past ten lessons, so you have a basic idea of how they work. Let's do a quick review of prepositions before we finish the book.

- Prepositions that indicate motion away from something generally take the genitive case. Examples: ἀπό, ἐκ/ἐξ

- Prepositions that show something or someone is staying in one place generally take the dative case. Example: ἐν

- Prepositions that show movement toward something generally take the accusative case. Examples: πρός, εἰς

Greek prepositions can be tricky at times. A preposition can have one meaning when it takes the genitive case, another meaning with the dative case, and yet another meaning with the accusative case! And, just as in English, prepositions can show all kinds of different relationships in time and space, and even in abstract concepts and ideas. Also (and this is a big deal in Greek) prepositions can be prefixed to verbs in ways that change a verb's meaning. So as you go along, remember the guidelines I have taught you, but at the same time be ready to learn much more about Greek prepositions.

230

GENERAL ADVICE

Congratulations! You have made it all the way to the end of this book. In closing, I would like to offer a few thoughts which you, the reader, may find helpful. These tips and observations should prove useful as you continue your study of ancient Greek.

First, a translation tip: When translating Greek, your mind must be awake and alert. Why? Because ancient Greek sentences can often be like jigsaw puzzles that you must put together. Your mind should analyze and process each word, trying to arrive at the correct way to fit that word in with the other words of the sentence. This can be difficult at first, but you will improve gradually with practice.

Greek not only improves one's knowledge of English vocabulary, but also sharpens the mind by building logical thinking skills. In addition, learning ancient Greek builds awareness of grammatical and linguistic concepts. The knowledge you gain from your efforts will benefit you as you approach other subjects such as English, history, philosophy, and religion.

Another tip: Someone who is accustomed to running a distance of only one or two miles probably will not suddenly try to run a marathon. It is the same with ancient Greek. Don't frustrate yourself by trying to read something that is much too difficult for you. In more advanced Greek, the sentences may be quite long and complicated. Also, there may be words and grammatical structures that you have not studied yet. Of course, it is good to give yourself a challenge, but not something so difficult that you end up feeling discouraged. Therefore, try to read texts that are on your reading level.

Please take a moment to reflect on all you have learned. Although you have come a long way from lesson 1, there is still much to learn. I hope this book has been enjoyable and profitable for you, and that the things you have learned from this book will become the foundation of a lifetime of enjoyment of the Greek language.

ANSWER KEY

LESSON 7

1. bet
2. let
3. bell
4. belt
5. tell

LESSON 8

1. led
2. debt
3. dell
4. bed
5. belt
6. tell
7. let
8. bell

LESSON 9

1. fell
2. left
3. fed
4. deaf
5. felt
6. bell
7. led
8. debt
9. belt
10. bet

LESSON 10

1. boat
2. load
3. loaf
4. float
5. fellow
6. photo
7. left
8. led
9. felt
10. fed

LESSON 11

1. phone
2. net
3. tone
4. note
5. lone/loan
6. bone
7. fellow
8. loaf
9. fed
10. boat
11. debt
12. load

LESSON 12

1. sell
2. boats
3. toast
4. sled
5. boast
6. set
7. best
8. dose
9. nest
10. snow
11. dead
12. left
13. tone
14. fed
15. photo

LESSON 13

1. cone
2. soak
3. neck
4. coat
5. code
6. coast
7. decks
8. nets

9. toast
10. loaf
11. photo
12. sled
13. nest
14. phone
15. sell

LESSON 14

1. goat
2. leg
3. ghost
4. guess
5. egg
6. goats
7. logo
8. bed
9. set
10. dose
11. nest
12. fed
13. boast
14. float
15. snow

LESSON 15

1. comb
2. melt
3. dome
4. foam
5. melts
6. mode
7. most
8. smell
9. leg
10. load
11. guess
12. nest
13. cone
14. goal
15. fed

LESSON 16

1. pet
2. soap
3. pest
4. cope
5. sled
6. float
7. ghost
8. nest
9. foam
10. fled
11. most
12. goats
13. neck
14. deaf
15. leg

LESSON 17

1. hotel
2. elbow
3. oaks
4. hoax
5. host
6. home
7. elm
8. helm
9. hope
10. head
11. pope
12. ghost
13. phone
14. guess
15. note
16. photo
17. bone
18. soaps

LESSON 18

1. both
2. oath
3. tenth
4. depth
5. death
6. head
7. helm
8. elbow
9. oaks
10. host
11. home
12. elm
13. hope
14. hotel
15. logo
16. phone
17. step
18. toast

LESSON 19

1. oaks
2. necks
3. oaks
4. necks
5. hoax
6. oath
7. pokes
8. pokes
9. soaks
10. soaks
11. hope
12. melts
13. pest
14. elbow
15. fed
16. goal
17. nests
18. both

LESSON 20

1. hopes
2. hopes
3. mopes
4. mopes
5. soaps
6. soaps
7. oaks
8. both
9. tenth
10. death
11. oath
12. ghost
13. depth
14. next
15. helm
16. soap
17. cope
18. guest

LESSON 21

1. taco
2. dot
3. hot
4. lot
5. pot
6. tenth
7. hopes
8. pokes
9. soaps
10. oath
11. helm
12. soaks
13. mopes
14. beg
15. depth
16. oaks
17. both
18. necks

LESSON 22

1. hot taco
2. both guests
3. left leg
4. hoax photo
5. hotel bed
6. boats float
7. head home
8. snow melts
9. cell phone
10. pet goat
11. tenth step
12. elbow bone
13. next snow
14. bell tone
15. oak boat
16. best soaps
17. tenth taco
18. hot toast
19. dead phone
20. home debt
21. foam soap
22. boat load
23. goat smell
24. snow sled
25. leg bone
26. nest egg
27. phone home
28. hot pot
29. snow cone
30. hotel logo

LESSON 34

1. boy
2. sky
3. cloud
4. fly
5. foil
6. loud
7. tie
8. scout
9. cow
10. toy
11. fine
12. down

LESSON 35

1. queen
2. goose
3. fate
4. sweet
5. late
6. tweet
7. loom
8. skate
9. sweep
10. tool
11. fine
12. cow
13. tie
14. sky
15. down
16. boy
17. cloud
18. toy
19. foil
20. scoot
21. fly

LESSON 36

1. *hoist*
2. *week/weak*
3. *high*
4. *house*
5. *hoop*
6. *out*
7. *how*
8. *ice*
9. *weep*
10. *height*
11. *howl*
12. *fate*
13. *fly*
14. *queen*
15. *boy*
16. *sweet*
17. *toy*
18. *goose*
19. *sweep*
20. *loom*
21. *scoot*
22. *tie*
23. *cow*
24. *loud*
25. *tool*
26. *late*
27. *cloud*
28. *fine*
29. *foil*
30. *tweet*

LESSON 43

1. *the teacher*
2. *a teacher*
3. *the farmer*
4. *a farmer*

LESSON 44

1. he (takes the place of *Alfred*)
2. it (takes the place of *locker room*)
3. she
4. they (takes the place of *kids*)
5. he (takes the place of *Johnny*)
6. we
7. they
8. you
9. it (takes the place of *rabbit*)
10. they (takes the place of *children*)

LESSON 45

1. *I am.*
2. *I am a teacher.*
3. *I am the teacher.*
4. *I am a farmer.*
5. *I am the farmer.*

LESSON 46

1. *I am.*
2. *I am Alexander.*
3. *I am Cadmus.*
4. *I am Telemachus.*
5. *I am a farmer.*
6. *I am the farmer.*
7. *I am a teacher.*
8. *I am the teacher.*

LESSON 47

1. *I am.*
2. *I am Alexander.*
3. *I am Cadmus.*
4. *I am the farmer.*
5. *I am Telemachus.*

6. *I am a teacher.*
7. *I am Cadmus.*
8. *I am a farmer.*
9. *I am the teacher.*
10. *I am Telemachus.*

LESSON 50

1. *I am.*
2. *I am a farmer.*
3. *I am a farmer.*
4. *I am a teacher.*
5. *I am the teacher.*
6. *I am the farmer.*
7. *I am the teacher.*
8. *I am Telemachus.*
9. *I am Cadmus.*
10. *I am Alexander.*

LESSON 53

1. *I am a doctor.*
2. *I am the doctor.*
3. *I am a farmer.*
4. *I am the farmer.*
5. *I am Alexander.*
6. *I am the teacher.*
7. *I am Telemachus.*
8. *I am Cadmus.*
9. *I am Telemachus.*
10. *I am Alexander.*

LESSON 54

1. *I am a philosopher.*
2. *I am the philosopher.*
3. *I am a philosopher.*
4. *I am the philosopher.*
5. *I am a farmer.*
6. *I am Telemachus.*
7. *I am the teacher.*
8. *I am Cadmus.*
9. *I am Alexander.*
10. *I am the doctor.*

LESSON 55

1. I
2. you
3. she
4. Fred
5. Chicago
6. children
7. car
8. oatmeal
9. Switzerland
10. Grandfather

LESSON 56

1. subject: she
   verb: walks
2. subject: car
   verb: is
3. subject: I
   verb: see
4. subject: he
   verb: bought
5. subject: Sam
   verb: loves
6. subject: they
   verb: swim
7. subject: books
   verb: are
8. subject: I
   verb: called
9. subject: China
   verb: produces
10. subject: dog
    verb: barks

LESSON 57

1. *I am a philosopher and a doctor.*
2. *I am the teacher and the doctor.*
3. *I am Cadmus.*
4. *I am Telemachus.*
5. *I am the farmer.*
6. *I am a farmer and a philosopher.*
7. *I am a philosopher and a doctor.*
8. *I am Cadmus.*
9. *I am a doctor.*
10. *I am Alexander.*

LESSON 58

1. *I am not.*
2. *I am not Alexander.*
3. *I am not a philosopher.*
4. *I am not a doctor.*
5. *I am a doctor and a teacher.*
6. *I am not Cadmus.*
7. *I am a farmer.*
8. *I am not a teacher.*
9. *I am Telemachus.*
10. *I am Cadmus.*

LESSON 59

1. *You are not Cadmus.*
2. *You are a doctor.*
3. *You are a doctor.*
4. *You are a farmer and a teacher.*
5. *I am not a philosopher.*
6. *I am Alexander.*
7. *I am not Telemachus.*
8. *You are a philosopher.*
9. *I am not Cadmus.*
10. *I am a philosopher and a doctor.*

LESSON 61

1. *Alexander is a teacher.*
2. *Telemachus is a doctor.*
3. *Cadmus is not a farmer.*
4. *The farmer is not a doctor.*
5. *You are a doctor.*
6. *I am not Telemachus.*
7. *You are not Cadmus.*
8. *I am a farmer and a teacher.*
9. *The philosopher is a teacher.*
10. *You are not a doctor.*

LESSON 62

1. *I am the general.*
2. *I am a general.*
3. *I am the general.*
4. *I am a general.*
5. *Alexander is the general.*
6. *You are not a general.*
7. *The doctor is not a farmer.*
8. *Cadmus is not a general.*
9. *Telemachus is a doctor and a teacher.*
10. *The philosopher is not a doctor.*

LESSON 63

1. car (singular)
2. we (plural)
3. flowers (plural)
4. I (singular)
5. they (plural)
6. Jimmy (singular)
7. team (singular)
8. Mary (singular)
9. they (plural)
10. houses (plural)

LESSON 64

1. *farmer*
2. *farmers*
3. *teacher*
4. *teachers*
5. *doctor*
6. *doctors*
7. *philosopher*
8. *philosophers*
9. *general*
10. *generals*

LESSON 65

1. *The farmer*
2. *The farmers*
3. *The doctor*
4. *The doctors*
5. *The teacher and the farmers*
6. *The general is a philosopher.*
7. *You are a teacher and a philosopher.*
8. *I am not a farmer.*
9. *Cadmus is a general.*
10. *Telemachus is not a general.*

LESSON 66

1. *We are.*
2. *We are not the farmers.*
3. *We are farmers.*
4. *We are not the doctors.*
5. *We are teachers and doctors.*
6. *Cadmus is not a general.*
7. *You are not Telemachus.*
8. *I am a general and a philosopher.*
9. *Alexander is the general.*
10. *The general is a farmer.*

LESSON 67

1. *Y'all are.*
2. *Y'all are teachers.*
3. *Y'all are doctors.*
4. *Y'all are the philosophers.*
5. *We are not teachers.*
6. *We are not the doctors.*
7. *You are the general.*
8. *Telemachus is a teacher and a philosopher.*
9. *I am not a farmer.*
10. *Cadmus is not a farmer.*

LESSON 68

1. *The teachers are doctors.*
2. *Telemachus and Alexander are not doctors.*
3. *The philosophers are teachers.*
4. *We are generals.*
5. *Y'all are not farmers.*
6. *The doctor is a farmer.*
7. *Cadmus is a teacher.*
8. *You are not a general.*
9. *Alexander is not a teacher.*
10. *We are farmers.*

LESSON 69

1. I (first person singular)
2. you (second person singular)
3. she (third person singular)
4. we (first person plural)
5. y'all (second person plural)
6. they (third person plural)

7. he (third person singular)
8. it (third person singular)
9. y'all (second person plural)
10. flowers (third person plural)

LESSON 72

1. *I*
2. *I am.*
3. *I am.*
4. *I am Alexander.*
5. *I am Cadmus.*
6. *I am a philosopher.*
7. *Y'all are the doctors.*
8. *Telemachus and Alexander are not teachers.*
9. *We are not philosophers.*
10. *Cadmus is not the general.*

LESSON 73

1. *you*
2. *You are Telemachus.*
3. *You are not a farmer.*
4. *I am a general.*
5. *Cadmus is a doctor.*
6. *Alexander is not a doctor.*
7. *The farmer is not a general.*
8. *Y'all are not teachers.*
9. *We are teachers and philosophers.*
10. *Alexander and Telemachus are teachers.*

LESSON 74

1. we
2. We are.
3. We are.
4. We are.
5. We are farmers.
6. Y'all are teachers.
7. The farmers are not generals.
8. You are a doctor and a teacher.
9. I am a philosopher.
10. The general is a philosopher.

LESSON 75

1. y'all
2. Y'all are farmers.
3. We are doctors.
4. Y'all are not philosophers.
5. The generals are not doctors.
6. Cadmus is a teacher.
7. Telemachus is a farmer and a general.
8. The doctor is not a farmer.
9. I am not Alexander.
10. You are a general.

LESSON 76

1. I am not a merchant.
2. We are merchants.
3. Telemachus and Alexander are merchants.
4. You are a general.
5. Cadmus is not the doctor.
6. I am Alexander.
7. Y'all are farmers.

8. The generals are not philosophers.
9. You are not a merchant.
10. Alexander is a general.

LESSON 79

1. I am running OR I run.
2. I am running OR I run.
3. I am running OR I run.
4. You are a merchant.
5. We are merchants.
6. The general is a farmer.
7. The philosophers are doctors.
8. We are merchants and farmers.
9. Alexander and Cadmus are not generals.
10. Y'all are teachers.

LESSON 80

1. I am not.
2. I am not running.
3. I am not running.
4. Y'all are not teachers.
5. Telemachus is not a philosopher.
6. The merchants are not philosophers.
7. We are not doctors.
8. Y'all are doctors and teachers.
9. The general is not a doctor.
10. You are not a farmer.

LESSON 81

1. You are running.
2. You are running.
3. You are not running.
4. I am running.

5. We are doctors and teachers.
6. You are not Cadmus.
7. The merchant is a general.
8. Y'all are farmers.
9. The philosophers are doctors and teachers.
10. We are philosophers.

LESSON 82

1. The philosopher is running.
2. Cadmus is not running.
3. You are running.
4. I am not running.
5. We are not teachers.
6. Telemachus and Cadmus are merchants.
7. Y'all are doctors.
8. The farmer is a philosopher.
9. The teachers are not generals.
10. I am a farmer.

LESSON 83

1. We are running.
2. We are not running.
3. Alexander is running.
4. The merchant is running.
5. I am running.
6. We are running.
7. Cadmus is not a doctor.
8. You are running.
9. We are philosophers and teachers.
10. Y'all are not generals.

LESSON 84

1. Y'all are running.
2. Telemachus is not running.
3. We are running.
4. The general is not a farmer.
5. Alexander is a doctor and a merchant.
6. Telemachus and Cadmus are farmers.
7. You are a teacher.
8. We are not the generals.
9. The doctors are philosophers.
10. I am running.

LESSON 85

1. They are running.
2. The teachers are not running.
3. Y'all are running.
4. Telemachus is running.
5. We are not the merchants.
6. The doctor is a farmer and a philosopher.
7. Alexander and Cadmus are generals.
8. We are running.
9. I am running.
10. You are running.

LESSON 87

1. Cadmus never runs.
2. You never run.
3. We never run.
4. The philosophers are farmers.
5. Alexander and Telemachus are running.
6. The teacher is a philosopher.
7. Y'all are running.
8. You are a farmer.
9. I never run.
10. Telemachus is a merchant.

LESSON 88

1. The horse is running.
2. We are not horses.
3. The horses are running.
4. The horse is not running.
5. We are running.
6. Alexander is a philosopher and a farmer.
7. The teachers are not farmers.
8. You never run.
9. I am running.
10. Y'all are running.

LESSON 90

1. We are not cats.
2. The cats are running.
3. The cat never runs.
4. Y'all are not cats.
5. You are not running.
6. The philosophers are doctors.
7. The horse never runs.
8. Telemachus is a teacher.
9. Y'all are running.
10. We are running.

LESSON 91

1. The cats run often.
2. The horse runs often.
3. I run often.
4. You never run.
5. Y'all are running.
6. We never run.
7. The cat never runs.
8. The merchant is a doctor.
9. We are generals.
10. Cadmus is a teacher.

LESSON 92

1. The cats sleep often.
2. The horses never sleep.
3. We are not sleeping.
4. Alexander sleeps often.
5. The cats never run.
6. Alexander is a merchant.
7. The general never runs.
8. Y'all sleep often.
9. You are sleeping.
10. The merchant is a general.

LESSON 93

1. I run often because I am a horse.
2. I sleep often because I am a cat.
3. We never run because we are generals.
4. Telemachus never runs.
5. The cat is sleeping.
6. The teachers never sleep.
7. Y'all are not running.
8. I am a doctor.
9. You never sleep.
10. Cadmus and Alexander are sleeping.

LESSON 95

1. I write often because I am a philosopher.
2. You never write because you are a cat.
3. We never sleep because we are farmers.
4. The merchant writes often.
5. The cats sleep often.
6. You never write because you are a horse.
7. We never run because we are generals.
8. The doctor is not running.
9. Alexander is not a merchant.
10. The teachers are sleeping.

LESSON 96

1. The farmer seldom sleeps.
2. Y'all seldom run because y'all are generals.
3. We seldom write because we are not philosophers.
4. The teachers are writing.
5. I never write because I am not a teacher.
6. Telemachus sleeps often because he is a cat.
7. We sleep often because we are cats.
8. Y'all are running.
9. You seldom sleep because you are a farmer.
10. The cats are running.

LESSON 97

1. I seldom read.
2. I never read because I am a cat.
3. The philosophers read often.
4. The philosopher reads often.
5. I am not running.
6. We write often because we are merchants.
7. The horses seldom run.
8. We sleep often because we are cats.
9. The general seldom sleeps.
10. We are merchants.

LESSON 98

1. The philosophers are reading and writing.
2. The teacher is writing and reading.
3. The merchant and the farmer are running.
4. Cadmus is a horse.
5. The doctor is reading and writing.
6. Y'all seldom sleep because y'all are farmers.
7. Alexander is a philosopher and a teacher.
8. Y'all are generals.
9. Y'all seldom write and read.
10. The philosopher is not a doctor.

LESSON 99

1. We are writing now.
2. The philosophers are reading now.
3. We are reading and writing now because we are teachers.
4. The merchant seldom sleeps.
5. Cadmus and Telemachus are sleeping.
6. The teacher writes often.
7. The horse and the cat are running.
8. You are not a doctor.
9. The philosophers are not doctors.
10. I am a farmer.

LESSON 100

1. The cats sleep every day.
2. I read every day because I am a philosopher.
3. We read and write every day because we are teachers.
4. We are sleeping now.
5. The farmers seldom sleep.
6. The farmer is a general.
7. The horses run often.
8. Telemachus reads often because he is a teacher.
9. I run every day.
10. The merchants are not farmers.

LESSON 101

1. newspaper
2. movie
3. trombone
4. baseball
5. fish
6. radio
7. building
8. speech
9. wallet
10. deer

LESSON 102

1. predicate nominative
2. direct object
3. direct object
4. direct object
5. direct object
6. predicate nominative
7. direct object
8. direct object
9. predicate nominative
10. predicate nominative

LESSON 103

1. ὁ γεωργός (subject)
2. ὁ γεωργός (predicate nominative)
3. τὸν γεωργόν (direct object)
4. ὁ γεωργός (subject)
5. τὸν γεωργόν (direct object)
6. ὁ γεωργός (predicate nominative)
7. ὁ γεωργός (subject)

LESSON 104

1. *I have a cat.*
2. *I am a cat.*
3. *You have the horse.*
4. *You are not a horse.*
5. *Cadmus has a horse because he is a farmer.*
6. *Y'all do not have the horse.*
7. *We have the cat now.*
8. *I sleep often because I am a cat.*
9. *Alexander seldom reads and writes.*
10. *The philosophers write every day.*

LESSON 105

1. *The pig is running.*
2. *I have the pig.*
3. *The pigs are sleeping now.*
4. *Cadmus has a pig and a horse because he is a farmer.*
5. *The pigs are running.*
6. *We never read because we are pigs.*
7. *The general seldom writes.*
8. *The teachers seldom sleep.*
9. *The merchant sleeps often.*
10. *We write and read every day.*

LESSON 106

1. *I have a pen.*
2. *The farmer does not have a pen.*
3. *The philosopher has a pen because he writes every day.*
4. *The farmers seldom write.*
5. *I do not have a cat because I am not a farmer.*
6. *The pigs run often.*
7. *The teachers read every day.*
8. *The horses never sleep.*
9. *The merchant is running.*
10. *I have a pig now.*

LESSON 107

1. *The farmers are chasing the pig.*
2. *The pig is chasing Telemachus now.*
3. *You chase the cat every day.*
4. *We never chase the cat.*
5. *Cadmus has a pen because he is a teacher.*
6. *Alexander is chasing Telemachus.*
7. *The horses and the pigs are chasing the farmer.*
8. *I do not have a horse because I am not a farmer.*
9. *Telemachus and Cadmus seldom read and write because they are not teachers.*
10. *We sleep often because we are cats.*

LESSON 110

1. *The farmer has a horse.*
2. *The farmer has horses.*
3. *The farmer has the horse.*
4. *The farmer has the horses.*
5. *The cat chases the pigs every day.*
6. *The philosopher has the pens.*
7. *I do not have horses because I am not a farmer.*
8. *The generals do not have horses.*
9. *We seldom read.*
10. *Telemachus is chasing the pigs now.*

LESSON 111

1. *The merchants are buying pigs.*
2. *We never buy horses because we are not farmers.*
3. *The philosopher is buying the pens.*
4. *The merchant is chasing the pig.*
5. *Alexander reads every day because he is a philosopher.*
6. *Y'all have pens because y'all are philosophers.*
7. *The teacher is writing and reading now.*
8. *Telemachus is chasing Alexander.*
9. *I buy pens every day because I am a teacher.*

10. *Cadmus is sleeping.*

LESSON 112

1. *Cadmus has the bread.*
2. *We have bread because we are farmers.*
3. *The philosophers seldom buy bread.*
4. *The cats are sleeping.*
5. *The doctor is chasing the farmer.*
6. *The teachers buy pens often.*
7. *I do not have horses because I am not a farmer.*
8. *The merchant buys pigs often.*
9. *We are chasing the pigs.*
10. *I seldom write because I do not have a pen.*

LESSON 113

1. *The cats are always sleeping.*
2. *The teachers always have pens because they write every day.*
3. *Telemachus always has horses because he is a farmer.*
4. *We never buy pigs because we are not merchants.*
5. *The pig is chasing the cats.*
6. *We sleep often because we are cats.*
7. *The merchants are chasing the doctor.*
8. *The cats are sleeping.*
9. *Y'all do not have bread.*
10. *We never read because we are not philosophers.*

LESSON 114

1. *I never eat bread.*
2. *Cadmus seldom eats bread.*
3. *I buy and eat bread every day.*
4. *Y'all always eat bread.*
5. *The farmers have horses.*
6. *The cat is chasing the pigs.*
7. *Alexander does not have a cat.*
8. *The farmer has the horses and the pigs.*
9. *We are buying a pen now.*
10. *I buy horses often because I am a merchant.*

241

LESSON 115

1. The cooks do not have a pig.
2. Cadmus is a cook.
3. The cook buys pigs often.
4. Telemachus is chasing the pig because he is a cook.
5. The horses are sleeping now.
6. Y'all seldom run because y'all are generals.
7. I eat bread often.
8. Alexander is not a doctor.
9. I do not have a pen.
10. We always sleep because we are cats.

LESSON 117

1. The philosophers never have gold.
2. I seldom have gold because I am a farmer.
3. The merchants always have gold.
4. The cooks are chasing the pigs.
5. You never buy pens because you never write.
6. I have a pen because I write every day.
7. The horses are sleeping now.
8. Y'all are merchants.
9. You read and write every day because you are a doctor.
10. I always eat the bread.

LESSON 118

1. The farmer always has butter and cheese.
2. I never eat cheese.
3. I often eat bread and butter.
4. Alexander never buys butter because he is a farmer.
5. The cat is eating the cheese.
6. The cooks are chasing Telemachus because he has the cheese and the bread.
7. You do not have the pens.

8. I always have gold because I am a merchant.
9. You buy butter every day because you are a cook.
10. I am sleeping now.

LESSON 119

1. I do not have silver because I am a philosopher.
2. Telemachus and Cadmus are chasing the merchants because they have gold and silver.
3. I have the silver.
4. The cook is chasing the pig.
5. The generals have gold and silver.
6. Y'all are cats.
7. We seldom eat butter because we are not farmers.
8. Telemachus always has gold because he is a merchant.
9. We buy cheese and butter every day.
10. I seldom sleep because I am a farmer.

LESSON 121

1. The cat is eating the cook's bread.
2. You have Telemachus's silver.
3. The cook's cat is eating the cheese.
4. We are chasing Cadmus's cats.
5. I buy butter often because I am a cook.
6. We always have pens because we are teachers.
7. The cook chases the pigs often.
8. Alexander's horses run often.
9. Telemachus has gold and silver because he is a merchant.
10. The doctor's horse is eating the butter.

LESSON 122

1. Telemachus has a son.
2. The farmer's sons are chasing the pig.
3. We are chasing Cadmus's sons.
4. The farmer's cat is eating the butter.
5. We always read because we are philosophers.
6. The cooks have the gold.
7. I never eat cheese.
8. The farmer's horses are running.
9. Y'all always have gold and silver because y'all are merchants.
10. The cook is eating the bread.

LESSON 123

1. We never eat the farmers' cheese.
2. The cooks buy the farmers' butter every day.
3. We do not have the teachers' pens.
4. Alexander has the generals' gold.
5. We do not have the merchants' silver.
6. I do not have the philosopher's pens.
7. I eat often because I am a pig.
8. Telemachus seldom writes because he is not a teacher.
9. Alexander's son is a cook.
10. The philosophers always read.

LESSON 124

1. The cook's brother is chasing the pig.
2. Cadmus's brothers are merchants.
3. Alexander's brother never has silver because he is a teacher.
4. The merchant is chasing Telemachus's brother.
5. We are chasing the farmers' horses.
6. Cadmus's cats are eating the cooks' cheese.
7. The farmers' sons never sleep.
8. Y'all are not doctors.
9. We have pigs because we are farmers.
10. The merchant's son eats bread and butter every day.

LESSON 125

1. The teacher is teaching.
2. The teachers are teaching.
3. I teach because I am a teacher.
4. The philosopher is teaching Alexander's sons.
5. The teacher is teaching Alexander and Cadmus.
6. We teach Telemachus's sons every day.
7. Cadmus teaches often because he is a teacher.
8. Y'all buy the cooks' butter every day.
9. Telemachus's brother is chasing the cats.
10. I am sleeping now.

LESSON 126

1. Alexander's uncles are merchants.
2. Telemachus's uncle has horses and pigs because he is a farmer.
3. The cook's uncle always has cheese.
4. You have silver and gold often because you are a merchant.
5. Cadmus is chasing the farmers' pigs.
6. I never teach because I am not a teacher.
7. Alexander's brother never eats butter.
8. The farmers' horses seldom sleep.
9. Cadmus's son reads and writes often.
10. The cats sleep often.

LESSON 128

1. direct object: *money*
   indirect object: *friend*
2. direct object: *money*
   indirect object: *charity*
3. direct object: *example*
   indirect object: *class*
4. direct object: *curtains*
   indirect object: *house*
5. direct object: *seeds*
   indirect object: *garden*
6. direct object: *sandwiches*
   indirect object: *us*
7. direct object: *story*
   indirect object: *judge*
8. direct object: *song*
   indirect object: *audience*
9. direct object: *copies*
   indirect object: *everyone*
10. direct object: *shirt*
    indirect object: *me*

LESSON 130

1. *I am giving the cheese to the farmer.*
2. *I am giving gold and silver to the merchant.*
3. *I seldom give cheese to the cook.*
4. *I am not giving the pens to Alexander.*
5. *I am not giving bread to Cadmus's son.*
6. *You teach every day because you are a teacher.*
7. *The cook's uncle is a farmer.*
8. *I am buying the farmers' horses.*
9. *The farmer's brother always has cheese and butter.*
10. *The doctor's sons are chasing the cat.*

LESSON 131

1. *I am giving fodder to the horse.*
2. *The horses do not have fodder.*
3. *Every day I give fodder to the pig because I am a farmer.*
4. *The pigs and the horses have fodder.*
5. *The cat is eating the horse's fodder.*
6. *We have fodder because we are horses.*
7. *I buy pens every day because I am a philosopher.*
8. *The philosopher's cat is eating the cheese.*
9. *Cadmus often teaches the merchants' sons.*
10. *The brother and uncle of Alexander are doctors.*

LESSON 132

1. *I often give bread to Cadmus's sons.*
2. *I am giving the pigs to the farmers.*
3. *I am giving pens to the philosophers and the teachers.*
4. *Every day I give fodder to the horses because I am a farmer.*
5. *I never give silver to Alexander's uncle.*
6. *Cadmus often eats bread and butter.*
7. *We never teach because we are not teachers.*
8. *The doctor's brothers are philosophers.*
9. *I have the teachers' pens.*
10. *The pig is eating the horses' fodder.*

LESSON 133

1. *I am giving the fields to the farmer.*
2. *I am giving the field to Alexander.*
3. *We have a field because we are farmers.*
4. *I am giving cheese to the sons of Cadmus.*
5. *Telemachus and Cadmus do not have fields because they are not farmers.*
6. *The merchant always has gold and silver.*
7. *We teach the doctors' sons every day.*
8. *Cadmus's uncles are generals.*
9. *The farmer's cats are not eating the fodder.*
10. *The teachers eat bread and butter every day.*

LESSON 134

1. *The philosopher does not have a house.*
2. *The farmers have fields and houses.*
3. *Y'all do not have a house.*
4. *We are buying Cadmus's house.*
5. *I do not have a house because I am a philosopher.*
6. *The brothers of Cadmus are teachers.*
7. *The cook always buys cheese and butter.*
8. *The pig is chasing Alexander's cat.*
9. *I never give fodder to the cats.*
10. *The philosophers seldom teach the farmers' sons.*

LESSON 135

1. *Alexander, you are not a cook.*
2. *Horses, y'all have fodder.*
3. *Cat, you are always sleeping.*
4. *Cadmus, you are not a philosopher.*
5. *Philosophers, y'all do not have houses.*
6. *Cadmus's son is Telemachus's uncle.*
7. *I seldom eat bread.*
8. *Alexander and Telemachus are teaching the merchants' sons.*
9. *Cadmus does not have a field because he is not a farmer.*
10. *I am giving fodder to the horses.*

LESSON 138

1. *You never give gold to the brothers of Telemachus.*
2. *You are giving bread to the farmer's son.*
3. *Farmers, I often give bread to the pigs.*
4. *General, you do not have a horse.*
5. *Every day I buy the merchants' butter and cheese.*
6. *The farmers have fields and houses.*
7. *I often give bread to the teacher's sons.*
8. *Cadmus, you are not a general.*
9. *Alexander's horses do not have fodder.*
10. *We never run because we are generals.*

LESSON 139

1. *The farmer is giving fodder to the pigs.*
2. *The philosopher is giving the pen to the teacher.*
3. *You are giving the bread to the cook's son.*
4. *You are giving the field to the farmers because they do not have fields.*
5. *Cadmus's uncle never has gold.*
6. *The merchant is giving bread to the philosophers.*
7. *The doctor has cats.*
8. *I am sleeping now because I am a cat.*
9. *Philosopher, you do not have a house.*
10. *The farmers are chasing the horses.*

LESSON 140

1. *We never give butter to the merchants.*
2. *We often give bread to the sons of Telemachus.*
3. *Cadmus's brother is giving the pigs to the farmer.*
4. *Son, you are not a general.*
5. *Alexander chases the farmers' horses every day.*
6. *Cadmus and Telemachus do not have a house because they are philosophers.*
7. *Brother, you are not a cook.*
8. *The farmer is giving the fields to Alexander.*
9. *Cadmus's uncle is always sleeping.*
10. *The cats are always sleeping.*

LESSON 141

1. *Y'all often give fodder to the horses because y'all are farmers.*
2. *Y'all never give gold to Cadmus's uncle.*
3. *We give bread and butter to the philosophers every day because they do not have bread.*
4. *The general is giving the house to Alexander.*
5. *You are giving silver to the merchants' sons.*
6. *The philosophers are teaching Telemachus's brothers.*
7. *The merchant is buying the field.*
8. *We have pigs and horses because we are farmers.*
9. *I seldom eat cheese.*
10. *Cadmus, you are not a general.*

LESSON 142

1. *The farmer's sons are giving cheese and butter to the cooks.*
2. *The general is giving gold to the merchant.*
3. *Y'all are giving pens to Alexander.*
4. *We never give fodder to the horses because we are not farmers.*
5. *Cadmus's brother is giving the fields to the farmers.*
6. *You are giving the pens to the philosophers.*
7. *Alexander's uncles are not doctors.*
8. *The horses never read.*
9. *I teach the son of the merchant every day because I am a teacher.*
10. *The farmer's cat is chasing the pigs.*

LESSON 144

1. Preposition: *behind*
   Object of preposition: *couch*
2. Preposition: *beside*
   Object of preposition: *lamp*
3. Preposition: *in*

Object of preposition: *trunk*
4. Preposition: *through*
   Object of preposition: *tunnel*
5. Preposition: *under*
   Object of preposition: *house*
6. Preposition: *before*
   Object of preposition: *lunch*
7. Preposition: *after*
   Object of preposition: *school*
8. Preposition: *by*
   Object of preposition: *post office*
9. Preposition: *on*
   Object of preposition: *campus*
10. Preposition: *beyond*
    Object of preposition: *mountain*

LESSON 149

1. *The pig is in the house.*
2. *The horse is in the field.*
3. *The farmer is not in the house.*
4. *The cats are in the house.*
5. *The merchant is giving the pig to the farmer.*
6. *The cats are sleeping in the house.*
7. *I never run in the house.*
8. *Cadmus is giving the pen to the teacher.*
9. *Horse, you are not a pig.*
10. *We are giving bread to Alexander because he does not have bread.*

LESSON 150

1. *Cadmus's pig is in the river.*
2. *The farmers' sons are in the river.*
3. *The horses are in the rivers.*
4. *Cadmus's son is in the house.*
5. *Cadmus and Alexander are in the river.*
6. *You are giving the gold to the merchants.*
7. *The philosophers are reading in the house.*
8. *Telemachus's uncle is a general.*
9. *The pigs are in the fields.*
10. *We always give fodder to the horse.*

LESSON 151

1. Cadmus is running to the house.
2. The farmers' sons are running to the fields.
3. Telemachus and Alexander are running to the river.
4. The horses are running toward the farmer because he has fodder.
5. The farmer's son is in the river.
6. The fodder is in the field.
7. Cadmus is chasing the pig toward the houses.
8. Cat, you are always sleeping.
9. The farmers are giving fodder to the pigs now.
10. The teachers are teaching in the house.

LESSON 152

1. I walk to the river every day.
2. The farmer is walking to the field.
3. Alexander's sons are walking to the houses.
4. We never walk to the fields because we are not farmers.
5. Cadmus's uncle is sleeping in the house.
6. The farmer is chasing the pigs toward the field.
7. The horses are running toward the fields.
8. The pigs are in the houses.
9. I never buy the farmer's butter.
10. General, we do not have horses.

LESSON 153

1. I am walking from the house to the river.
2. We are walking from the river to the field.
3. Alexander is walking from the fields to the house.
4. The farmers are in the fields.

5. The general is giving a horse to Cadmus.
6. The cats are sleeping in the house.
7. The horses are running to the river.
8. Telemachus, you do not have a horse.
9. The farmer's son is running to the river.
10. Cat, you do not have fodder.

LESSON 154

1. Telemachus is walking to the woods.
2. The horse is in the woods.
3. The farmer's sons are walking to the woods.
4. We are walking from the woods to the river.
5. The pigs are running from the field to the woods.
6. The cats are running toward the houses.
7. Cadmus's uncle is sleeping in the woods.
8. Pig, you are not a horse.
9. The doctor is giving bread to Alexander's sons.
10. The cats are running from the pigs.

LESSON 155

1. The pigs are running into the woods.
2. Alexander's son is walking into the house.
3. Cadmus, we are walking into the woods.
4. The horses are running into the fields.
5. The farmers' sons are running into the house.
6. The general is in the woods.
7. The teacher is giving the pens to the philosophers.
8. We are not walking to the river.
9. The pig is running from the cook.
10. Cadmus and Alexander are walking from the woods to the river.

LESSON 156

1. *Alexander is walking from the house to the beach.*
2. *The horses are running to the beach.*
3. *Cadmus's brothers are walking from the beach to the woods.*
4. *I never walk to the beach.*
5. *We are walking into the woods.*
6. *The pig is sleeping in the house.*
7. *The merchants are walking from the beach to the river.*
8. *I often give bread to Alexander.*
9. *The gold is in the woods.*
10. *The farmer's son is running from the pigs.*

LESSON 157

1. *The horses are running out of the woods.*
2. *The farmer is walking out of the house toward the fields.*
3. *Telemachus is chasing the cat out of the house.*
4. *I never sleep in the woods.*
5. *The merchants walk to the beach every day.*
6. *Alexander is walking from the river to the house.*
7. *We are giving fodder to the horses because we are farmers.*
8. *You never walk to the beach.*
9. *The pig is running into the woods.*
10. *I am a farmer.*

THE GREEK ALPHABET

LETTER NAME	UPPERCASE	LOWERCASE	SOUND
alpha	Α	α	the *a* in *father*
beta	Β	β	the *b* in *boy*
gamma	Γ	γ	the *g* in *golf*
delta	Δ	δ	the *d* in *dog*
epsilon	Ε	ε	the *e* in *leg*
zeta	Ζ	ζ	the *sd* in *wisdom*
eta	Η	η	the *e* in *leg*
theta	Θ	θ	the *th* in *third*
iota	Ι	ι	the *i* in *machine*
kappa	Κ	κ	the *k* in *keep*
lambda	Λ	λ	the *l* in *log*
mu	Μ	μ	the *m* in *man*
nu	Ν	ν	the *n* in *now*
xi	Ξ	ξ	the *ks* in *sticks*
omicron	Ο	ο	the *o* in *hope*
pi	Π	π	the *p* in *pot*
rho	Ρ	ρ	a lightly rolled *r*
sigma	Σ	σ, ς	the *s* in *same*
tau	Τ	τ	the *t* in *top*
upsilon	Υ	υ	the *e* in *leg* but with rounded lips
phi	Φ	φ	the *ph* in *pharmacy*
chi	Χ	χ	a light scraping sound
psi	Ψ	ψ	the *ps* in *lips*
omega	Ω	ω	the *o* in *tone*

GREEK DIPHTHONGS

αι   Sounds like the vowel sound in *mine, fine,* and *pine.*

αυ   Sounds like the vowel sound in *how, now* and *cow.*

ει   It's a long story, but in this book we will pronounce it like the vowel sound in *eight.*

οι   Sounds like the vowel sound in *oil, foil,* and *toil.*

ου   Sounds like the vowel sound in *moose, loose* and *goose.*

υι   Sounds like the vowel sound in *queen, sweet* and *tweet.*

GLOSSARY

αἰγιαλός *beach*

αἴλουρος *cat*

ἀγοράζω *I buy*

ἀγρός *field*

ἀδελφός *brother*

ἀναγιγνώσκω *I read*

ἀπό *from*

ἄργυρος *silver*

ἄρτος *bread*

βαδίζω *I walk*

βούτῡρος *butter*

γεωργός *farmer*

γράφω *I write*

δρῡμός *woods*

διδάσκαλος *teacher*

διδάσκω *I teach*

διώκω *I chase*

δίδωμι *I give*

ἐγώ *I*

εἶ *you are*

εἰς *into*

εἰσί(ν) *they are*

εἰμί *I am*

ἐκ/ἐξ *out of*

ἔμπορος *merchant*

ἐν *in*

ἐσθίω *I eat*

ἐστέ *y'all are*

ἐστί(ν) *is, he is, she is, it is*

ἐσμέν *we are*

ἔχω *I have*

ἡμεῖς *we*

θεῖος *uncle*

ἰᾱτρός *doctor*

ἵππος *horse*

καί *and*

καθ' ἡμέραν *daily, every day*

καθεύδω *I sleep*

κάλαμος *reed-pen*

μάγειρος *cook*

νῦν *now*

ὁ *the*

οἶκος *house*

ὅτι *because*

οὐ/οὐκ/οὐχ *not*

οὔποτε *never*

πολλάκις *often*

πάντοτε *always*

ποταμός *river*

πρός *to, toward*

σπανίως *seldom*

στρατηγός *general*

σύ *you*

τρέχω *I run*

τῡρός *cheese*

υἱός *son*

ὑμεῖς *y'all*

φιλόσοφος *philosopher*

χοῖρος *pig*

χόρτος *fodder*

χρῡσός *gold*

251

Made in the USA
Middletown, DE
10 June 2023